DATE DUE

GAYLORD			PRINTED IN U.S.A.

The Truth of Uncertainty

The Truth of Uncertainty

Beyond Ideology in
Science and Literature

Edward L. Galligan

University of Missouri Press

COLUMBIA AND LONDON

Library of Congress Cataloging-in-Publication Data

Galligan, Edward L.
    The truth of uncertainty : beyond ideology in science and
literature / Edward L. Galligan.
        p.   cm.
    Includes bibliographical references and index.
    ISBN 0-8262-1192-5 (alk. paper)
    1. Criticism—Philosophy.   I. Title.
PN81.G24   1998
801'.95—dc21   98-8829
                                                          CIP

♾ ™ This paper meets the requirements of the American
National Standard for Permanence of Paper for Printed Library Materials,
Z39.48, 1984.

Text design: Elizabeth K. Young
Jacket design: Susan Ferber
Typesetter: Crane Composition
Printer and binder: Edwards Brothers, Inc.
Typefaces: Palatino, Helvetica 55 Roman, Helvetica 85 Heavy

This book has been subsidized with a grant from the Office of the
President, Western Michigan University, for which the University
of Missouri Press is grateful.

for Brownie
with love

No face which we can give to a matter will stead us so well at last as the truth. This alone wears well. For the most part, we are not where we are, but in a false position. Through an infirmity of our natures, we suppose a case, and put ourselves into it, and hence are in two cases at the same time, and it is doubly difficult to get out. In sane moments we regard only the facts, the case that is. Say what you have to say, not what you ought. Any truth is better than make-believe. Tom Hyde, the tinker, standing on the gallows, was asked if he had any thing to say. "Tell the tailors," said he, "to remember to make a knot in their thread before they take the first stitch." His companion's prayer is forgotten.

Henry David Thoreau, *Walden*

Contents

Preface

This book is not a critique of that collection of critical theories that swept over Anglo-American literary studies in the 1970s and 1980s, collectively known at first as Theory (always with that pretentious capitalization), then as poststructuralism, and now, frequently, as postmodernism. The demolition job has been done many times over, as it needed to be, and from many different points of view. I find particularly useful Colin Falck's devastating philosophical analysis in *Myth, Truth, and Literature,* Joseph Carroll's Darwinian critique in *Evolution and Literary Theory,* and Brian Vickers's careful, systematic dismantling of the various theories in *Appropriating Shakespeare;* but a number of other very good critics have contributed to the effort. Colin Falck thinks that the movement collapsed "with extreme suddenness" in 1989; I fear he's an optimist. Its acolytes are still coming out of graduate schools; its handsomely endowed professors are still publishing essays in well-known journals and books at university presses; and a person can still get in noisy trouble in a university faculty by offending postmodern sensibilities.

But if it is not a critique, it is a book that had its origins in my dismay over the quality of the thought and writing I discovered in postmodernist criticism when I retired from the English Department at Western Michigan University in January 1989 and too blithely assigned myself the task of catching up on what had been going on in the 1980s when administrative duties had been sopping up most of my time. A lot of the material for this book came out of reading and writing that I thought I was doing simply to express and justify that dismay. I generally prefer to avoid doing negative criticism, because it is so easy for it to turn into a smug demonstration of the critic's superiority to the work at hand and to its admirers. Perhaps for that reason, long before I thought I was working on a book, my concern was gradually shifting from the negative to the positive, from a rejection of criticism in the service of ideology to an affirmation of criticism in the service of truthfulness. I feel silly saying that, for I know that most critics have always taken it for granted that they were engaged in the search for truth and didn't bother bragging about it; but in this postmodern age when truth is so commonly held to be whatever anybody wants it to be, a sane man is well advised to make explicit his faith in the ideal of truthfulness.

So whatever it started out to be, this book is an exploration of the consequences for literary criticism of a full acceptance of Henry David Thoreau's doctrine that "any truth is better than make-believe." Almost immediately, it got me involved with the sciences, so much so that anybody glancing at the book is likely to be surprised by how heavily it draws on the work of people in physics, mathematics, biology, neurology, chemistry, and so forth and how little it has to do with works and ideas from the social sciences that postmodernist critics have cited and imitated, *ad nauseam*. But I am not a physicist or a biologist; I am a literary man, a creature of words and books, not of numbers and instruments, and my goal is to reach literary understandings. It's just that I was taught in literature classes to ask what the scientists were taught in laboratories to ask—what's the evidence?—and to reach whatever conclusions the evidence called for. Social scientists keep asking for data (a significantly different matter from asking for evidence) and freely—too freely to suit me—deal in generalizations of a sort that postmodernists find it easy to use.

This book emphatically is an essay, because I think it positively has to be. It's an essay in the sense that it is a trying out of some ideas, an exploration of some possibilities, a necessarily (not just politely) tentative piece. But it is also an essay in the sense that it is a personal and informal statement, not an impersonal, seemingly objective discourse. There are a number of good and sufficient reasons for that, but for now I will settle for one: reading, like all of the other work of consciousness, is a highly subjective enterprise; only a person, not a committee or a task force, can read a book, and though it may be disciplined in the interest of impartiality, a person's reading is naturally, inevitably—and perhaps even blessedly—subjective.

Acknowledgments

Nearly all of the reviews and essays that I have published in the last twenty years or so appeared in *The Sewanee Review;* they are the foundation on which this work is built. To its editor, George Core, I owe a special debt of gratitude.

I am legally obligated to acknowledge that Josef Skvorecky, George V. Higgins, and Edward Chalfant have given me permission to quote from the letters they have written to me, but my debts to them as storytellers and correspondents go far beyond legal niceties.

My friends and colleagues, especially Conrad Hilberry, Seamus Cooney, Katherine Joslin, and Tom Bailey, have been patient and helpful readers and listeners.

My wife has read and reread everything I have written with a sharp eye, a well-tuned ear, and a strong mind.

The Truth of Uncertainty

"Smile When You Say That, Pardner"

On December 1, 1987, the *New York Times* broke the story that Paul de Man, who at the time of his death four years earlier had been the leading deconstructionist critic in this country and a renowned, even revered professor at Yale University, had published pro-Nazi, anti-Semitic articles in the newspaper *Le Soir* and elsewhere in occupied Belgium in the period between December 1940, when the Germans were winning the war everywhere, and November 1942, when the Americans had landed in North Africa and the remnants of the German army that had attempted to capture Stalingrad surrendered to its Soviet defenders. For the rest of his life de Man kept quiet about those articles; they were discovered, ironically, by a diligent Belgian admirer of his who was doing what a good graduate student should and would do, checking in the library to see if he could find any early, uncollected works of the Master. That is not the sort of story that will fade away in a hurry; in fact, it grew as the months went on and more and more revelations came out concerning de Man's unsavory behavior during and after the war. It was still the subject of passionate debate when I retired and began my casual effort to catch up with what was going on in the world of criticism; it seemed like a good place to begin.

I was not wholly ignorant, of course. I knew about the collaborationist articles and had heard that de Man had abandoned a wife and children in Belgium when he came to this country in 1948; I also knew enough about deconstructionist ideas to realize that it was not entirely unjust to weigh the possibility that knowing about de Man's secrets should qualify our judgment of his published criticism and even of deconstructionism in general. I have long believed that scholars and critics ought to be held responsible for the public effects of their work just as other writers are, but mainly I thought this was a good excuse for reading a reasonable sample of what de Man and other deconstructionists, Jacques Derrida especially, had published. I was shocked to discover that I could not get anywhere—I mean that almost literally—with any of them. It's not that their ideas were so difficult, but that their writing was so bad, so deliberately vague and offensive, so plainly designed to keep all but true believers out of the discussion. I was not going to waste my time decoding stuff like that; I know my Orwell and I know that writing of that sort is, always, "the defense of the indefensible." It looked to me like they were all particularly anxious to defend a bad theory of language that they had gotten from—or perhaps foisted off on—Ferdinand de Saussure; so I dug out a translation of his *Course in General Linguistics* only to find that it was of very little help. Saussure was not deliberately obscure as they were, but the *Course* is based on a compilation of notes taken by people who had attended the three courses of lectures he gave at the University of Geneva between 1907 and 1911, and it suffers from the inevitable haziness of note takers trying to recapitulate demanding lectures. Even well-trained linguists differ on the interpretation of major aspects of Saussure's thinking. Though I am not a linguist of any sort, I do know that it does not make sense to say with Paul de Man, Derrida, and others that all use of language is indefinite and that consequently all statements are inconclusive. Not wanting, at least not at first, to put all my trust in what others were saying about Saussure, I went off looking for a theory of language that made sense in the light of my experience with it. I found what I needed in an essay of Walker Percy's, but before I go into that I think it would be best to stop worrying about the sequence in which I did things and summarize what I eventually learned from various clear-headed analysts of the linguistic ideas of de Man, Derrida, and their fellow postmodern theorists. It will be convenient to cite Colin Falck especially, because he has arranged his argument in a form that lends itself to summary; Brian Vickers and Joseph Carroll fully support Falck, but their much longer and much more complicated books defy quick summary.[1]

1. Colin Falck, *Myth, Truth, and Literature;* Brian Vickers, *Appropriating Shakespeare: Contemporary Critical Quarrels;* Joseph Carroll, *Evolution and Literary Theory.*

According to Falck, Saussure based his main arguments on two principles: the principle of the arbitrary nature of the sign, and the principle of the relational nature of all linguistic meaning. The first principle led him to argue that what he termed "the linguistic sign" unites "a concept and a sound-image" or, as he later put it, "the signifier and the signified." In practice this sensible, even traditional recognition of the arbitrariness of words led him on to the philosophically radical belief that the concepts were inherently arbitrary, too, that they were not formed by any extralinguistic relationship to reality. That assertion provided the basis for his second principle, the relational nature of all linguistic meaning, which led in turn to his argument that in language there are only differences, there are no independent, free-standing terms. Saussure understood very well that his propositions were aimed at the reform of language studies; the theorists who came along forty or fifty years later interpreted them as giving an incontestably sound account of the nature of language itself. That opened the barn door for them and they proceeded to take it for granted that language cannot be held to relate in any usefully discussable way to any extralinguistic dimension of reality. Great quantities of critical nonsense followed from that assumption, and it flowed unchecked because the theorists distorted another of Saussure's practical distinctions—between (roughly speaking) language as it exists in its culture, *langue,* and language as individuals use it, *parole*—enabling them to analyze language in the most abstract way possible without ever paying attention to the way we actually use it. Saussure cannot be blamed for such excesses, but he is responsible for strategies for studying language as though it were a disembodied phenomenon. Language is as hopelessly dependent on body, blood, and brains as human beings are, as even the most cerebral of critics are; any theory of language, such as the one Barthes, Derrida, and de Man based on a faulty understanding of Saussure's work, that does not begin with that fact and does not proceed to allow for and emphasize the role of evolution in the creation and the use of language, is hopelessly inadequate.

Falck is vigorous in his condemnation of the fallacy of Saussure's conclusion that no meaning-determining "presence" exists outside of language itself and offers a list of some eight false doctrines that the theorists have promulgated on the basis of the weird notion that a given piece of language, a "text," can mean whatever they say it can mean. But David Lehman delivers the most devastating critique of the doctrines of the theorists by noting what de Man's fellow deconstructionists said and wrote as they attempted to defend him from the charges raised by the discovery of his wartime writings, especially his essay titled "The Jews in Contemporary Literature."[2] To the rest of us, it looks like a piece of anti-Semitism, a fake-genteel, disgusting currying of favor with the Nazis; to his deconstructionist friends, of whom Jacques Derrida was by far the most verbose and devious, it looked at worst like a youthful folly, the sort of thing that was not at all uncommon among European intellectuals in the 1930s (Jonathan Culler) and at best like a skillfully subversive deconstruction of anti-Semitism itself (Derrida). "The approved deconstructive reading of 'The Jews in Contemporary Literature' would reduce it to an arena of contradictory impulses—this was the *reductio ad absurdum* of Paul de Man's theory of rhetoric," Lehman concluded. "What a curious irony that he had himself provided the posthumous text that would, when subjected to close analysis, demonstrate once and for all the danger of a rhetorical method that can be used to deny disagreeable truths—that can be used to deny *what is there.* One might even say that de Man's *Wartime Journalism* deconstructs the companion volume of *Responses*[3]—that what he actually wrote exposes the pretensions and the fallacies of the deconstructive commentary."[4] No wonder that one hears very little about de Man's critical writings these days, and that Jacques Derrida seems to be fading from sight and mind.

I wish I could say that when I turned away from the de Man affair to look for a sensible theory of language I had the sense to realize that I had been, in effect, acting on one during all the years that I pulled my brow low and proclaimed that I would rather have "a good ear for the language than all the analytical knowledge in the Linguistics Department of M.I.T.," but I felt I was fumbling in the dark until I found *The Message in the Bottle,* a stitched-together

2. Falck, *Myth,* 23–24; David Lehman, *Signs of the Times: Deconstruction and the Fall of Paul de Man;* Paul de Man, *Wartime Journalism, 1940–1942.*

3. Werner Hamacher, Neil Hertz, and Tom Keenan, eds., *Responses: On Paul de Man's Wartime Journalism.*

4. Lehman, *Signs,* 242.

collection of essays on the nature of human communication that Walker Percy had published between 1954 and 1975. Linguists and theorists have not paid as much attention to it as they should, perhaps because Percy was a good enough novelist to make his philosophical speculations look too simple to interest a specialist. Certainly he was a good enough novelist to know that language is not a matter of signs strung together according to a syntactical code of inexplicable origin, not a collection of linguistic bits that can be isolated in some mental test tube and subjected to something resembling a chemical analysis. He realizes that it is something far more subtle and mysterious: it is the means by which people talk to each other (and sometimes to themselves). You don't have to be American to understand that, but it seems to help.

Percy, who is fond of science fiction, imagines an intelligent being from Mars, one whose intelligence has evolved without language but, instead, by the development of extrasensory perception. The Martian, he thinks, would be astonished to discover that "earthlings *talk all the time* or otherwise traffic in symbols: gossip, tell jokes, argue, make reports, deliver lectures, listen to lectures, take notes, write books, read books, paint pictures, look at pictures, stage plays, attend plays, tell stories, listen to stories, cover blackboards with math symbols—and even at night dream dreams that are a very tissue of symbols. Earthlings in short seem to spend most of their time trafficking in one kind of symbol or another, while the other creatures of earth—more than two million species— *say not a word.*"[5]

When Percy's very reasonable Martian goes to earthling scientists to find out "what happens when people talk, when one person names something or says a sentence about something and another person understands him," he gets the runaround. Linguists can tell him about the history and grammatical structures of languages; psychologists can crank up not very persuasive learning theories for him and draw a lot of Stimulus-Response diagrams. Communication specialists and computer experts can tell him interesting and useful things about facilitating the flow of information in electronic circuits. Semiologists, who came along after Percy wrote his essay,

5. Walker Percy, *The Message in the Bottle: How Queer Man Is, How Queer Language Is, and What One Has to Do with the Other,* 12–13.

wouldn't have been of much more help. All their learned discourse about signs and referents is just another juggling of S-R diagrams, and they can't account for their own performances any better than the behavioral psychologists can. The Martian concludes "that earthlings for all their encyclopedic knowledge about the formal and factual aspects of language have managed to straddle the phenomenon itself and *miss* it."[6]

To begin to get some handle on the phenomenon itself, Percy turns away from his fantasy of the visiting Martian and considers the story of how Helen Keller came into possession of language one summer day when she was eight years old. She had already learned from her teacher, Miss Sullivan, how to use words as signs: if she tapped in Miss Sullivan's hand the signals for the letters *c-a-k-e*, Miss Sullivan would fetch a piece of cake for her. But that still left her locked in the isolation of her blind and deaf condition. Then one day Miss Sullivan tapped out *w-a-t-e-r* in her one hand while a stream of cool water gushed over her other hand. Somehow, God knows how, she suddenly realized that *w-a-t-e-r* meant that wonderful-feeling stuff flowing over her hand and also the similar stuff she had experienced before, drinking and bathing. Helen spent the rest of the day excitedly learning the names for the important phenomena in her life—*mother, father, sister, teacher,* and several others. The same miraculous thing happens to all children, though it is spread over so many days and weeks and occurs so naturally that we forget to see it as miraculous. Somehow, God knows how, the child realizes that when her father says "balloon" he means not only that particular object he has just puffed up but a lot of similar objects she has seen or will see. Very quickly she will have no trouble at all understanding that the pink rubbery thing that her father blew into, the shiny metallic thing that had to be held down with a weight at her birthday party to keep it from floating up to the ceiling, and the large, multicolored thing passing a few hundred feet in the air over her backyard are all equally and reasonably called *balloons*. These feats greatly impress Percy, as they should all of us.

No one possesses language alone. It takes two people to propagate it—Miss Sullivan to tap *w-a-t-e-r* into Helen's hand, a father to tell a child, "That's a balloon." But it also takes at least two people

6. Ibid., 15.

to use language, to exploit its power to transform life. For the young Helen Keller the discovery that *w-a-t-e-r* meant the same thing to Miss Sullivan and everyone else she knew as it did to her marked the end of solitary confinement; for the child the discovery that the word *balloon* has several rather different meanings both for her and for others is an amusingly complicated connection between herself and her world and her society. Language is *talk*, not mere speech or utterance; it is what we have in common with others of our kind and we jointly exploit it for all of the purposes, good and ill, known to social beings. It is saturated with meaning, more meaning than we can know, let alone control. The next sentence I hear or read might well have meaning that I have never heard before; the next one that I write or speak might have different implications for you and for me. Even at the level of the word it is never truly simple and at the level of the sentence it is practically always open to the possibility of different ways of understanding. It is inherently, necessarily, marvelously, exasperatingly ambiguous. That is why it can serve all of our purposes, both good and ill. It is beautifully crafted for the purpose of manipulating and hoodwinking others; it is equally beautifully crafted for the purpose of forging intellectual and emotional bonds with others. The price we pay for the possibility of whispering sweet nothings is the need to put up with a certain number of snake-oil salesmen; I trust that even a fierce deconstructionist would agree that sweet nothings are well worth the price.

All use of language is grounded in talk. If a speaker cannot hear how his statement should sound before he actually speaks it he will stammer incoherently; if a reader cannot hear how the sentence in front of him should sound if read aloud he will not make any sense of it. Everything that is written, from offhand notes to carefully polished essays, is a form of talk. For any given piece of writing the question is not whether it is grounded in talk but whether a reader can hear a voice saying it, and if so, whether it is speaking formally or informally. Bureaucrats are so exceedingly anxious to make it plain that they speak for their bureaus, not for themselves, that their prose frequently becomes unhearable and therefore incomprehensible. Presumably one or more actual living, breathing human beings were involved in writing the directions for completing the forms issued by the Internal Revenue Service, but you'd never know it from reading them. Educationists, mediocre social scientists, and run-of-the-mill followers of Saussure tend to write similarly unspeakable prose, partly in order to escape responsibility for what they are saying, partly because they think that it sounds more scientific and objective that way. Good scholars and thinkers, no matter what their discipline, command a careful, formal style of writing; any well-trained reader can hear voice in that prose—sometimes even a distinctly individual voice—but it is speaking deliberately, precisely. Though that is the effect that most academic writers aim to achieve, it is very hard to hit and they too often come out sounding stuffy, half-anesthetized. Other kinds of writers with other purposes—journalists, essayists, letter-writers, novelists, what have you—try to command a distinctly informal, casual, conversational style, but that's hard to do, too, and they come out sounding sloppy, half-baked. Yet it's all grounded in talk, some skillfully, some clumsily, but none of it is an exercise in sign painting.

Talk, I should note, is my term, not Percy's; it's a comfortably informal yet sufficiently accurate way of labeling the idea that he develops in carefully philosophical language in the later "chapters" of *The Message in the Bottle*. Having rejected all behavioristic theories of language on the grounds that very little of what happens in language can accurately be described in S-R diagrams, and having also rejected the various linguistic theories that describe it as a three-cornered, *triadic*, relationship involving a sign, an object of the sign, and an interpretant, he argues that language can only be understood if it is seen as *tetradic*—as the product of the efforts of two persons to communicate with each other a shared understanding of the relationship between what must be called a symbol, not a sign, and an object. His explanatory diagram is diamond-shaped: it shows one corner labeled "symbol" opposite another labeled "object," the two joined by a horizontal line labeled "Relation of Quasi-Identity"; the other two corners, representing the two persons, are joined by a vertical line marked "Relationship of Intersubjectivity." (Note the disciplined uncertainty in his labeling of both of those relationships.) The trouble is that at the time he was writing these essays no one had attempted a scientific study of the nature of language that took into account its tetradic complexity; the even worse trouble is that no one for a long time thereafter attempted such a study. The followers of the French Theorists blathered on with a dyadic notion of language and the followers of Noam Chomsky's version of linguistics resolutely pursued a triadic-based understanding of language and concentrated on syntactical analyses, largely ignoring the little problem of meaning. Neither group paid attention to Percy, even though—or possibly because—he offers exceedingly cogent critiques of their positions. Percy is too careful a thinker to claim that he has supplied an adequate theory of language, but he is properly confident that he has a firm grip on its essential nature. With all of his formal education in the sciences and somewhat less formal but still solid education in philosophy, Percy is comfortable with diagrams and with terms like *tetradic;* for my purposes here (and elsewhere, too, I must admit), *talk* is the clear and reliable term for the quality he is referring to.

What I have been saying so far applies to all languages everywhere and makes, as far as I can tell, good, sound sense—at least as much good, sound sense as can be made about a process whose central event remains shrouded in mystery. I have been staying close to the trunk of the tree, but now I want to go out on the end of a limb. I want to argue that American writing has special value not only for Americans but for people throughout the world, many of whom must read it in translations of frequently dubious accuracy, because it is so thoroughly and so happily soaked in the ways Americans talk to each other. I can't *prove* that our novelists, playwrights, screenwriters, and songwriters do things with the language of our talk that writers in other languages either cannot or will not do with their talk; I don't know enough about other languages. Nor can I *prove* that the effective representation of talk of all sorts supplies much of the attractive power of American writing. But it is true that the talk-filled forms of American writing have had astonishing pulling power, and it is reasonable to assume that our ways of talking—and we do talk a lot—have implications that we take so much for granted that we are rarely aware of them. My own guess is that the fundamental implication is that we feel free to talk like that.

Let's begin with some music, which Percy considers a form of symbolic expression closely related to language. American popular songs, the "standards" that jazz musicians love to play and to sing, have spread to practically every country in the world. The lyrics of nearly all of them are woven from common, idiomatic American talk. "Just One of Those Things," "But Not For Me," "Ain't Misbehavin'," "Old Rocking Chair's Got Me," "These Foolish Things," "My Bill," "Sweet Georgia Brown," "Easter Parade," "Saint Louis Woman," and hundreds of others have the great virtue of giving resonance and added meaning to the words, phrases, and notions that fill the talk of ordinary Americans. Only Americans can fully appreciate that effect, but ordinary people in other countries know, even if they are dealing with translated versions, that the songs glorify common speech and emotions. In cultures that have a long history of strong class distinctions, and in totalitarian countries where the state is attempting to impose rigid rules for what is permissible in speech, that can in itself have powerful appeal. Moreover, in playing and in singing these songs, performers are not merely permitted, they are practically required to supply their own individual interpretations. Ira Gershwin's lyrics carry one set of meanings when Ella Fitzgerald sings "But Not For Me" and a distinctly different set when Rosemary Clooney sings it; George Gershwin's music for that wonderful song goes through similar changes when Jimmy Rowles plays it on his piano and Dave McKenna on his. The jazz standards are *standards* because they succeed in serving the needs of people everywhere for self-expression—not all people in every place, but all sorts of people in all sorts of places. No wonder both the Nazis and the Communists hated jazz; they could neither understand nor control it. You can turn that around, too: one of the big reasons for loving jazz is that the bastards can't control it.

Though I am reasonably sure I am right, I can understand a skeptical response to my claim of worldwide popularity for American jazz. But the enormous popularity of American movies—especially of Westerns and of their offspring, hard-boiled detective and gangster movies—is beyond the doubt of even a professional doubter. How could anybody childish enough to like movies at all fail to delight in movies that deliver hour after hour of vivid, emotionally affecting action culminating in a symbolically significant triumph for the good guys? Violent action makes them tick, but some part of the appeal of these movies is linguistic—the wisecracks of the hard-boiled detective, the racy slang of the cops and the gangsters, and the laconic observations of the Western hero. I was very lucky as a movie-goer: the first one I remember seeing was *The Virginians* with Gary Cooper (who was the ideal good guy of Westerns) and Walter Huston (who was actor enough to make the bad guy perfectly credible). Even a six-year-old could relish both its action and its talk: the ending in which the bad guy loses his shootout with Coop and falls dead into the dusty street, and that great moment earlier in the movie when Coop delivers his warning to the bad guy, "Smile when you say that, pardner."

I discovered a few years later that the movie was based on a novel by somebody named Owen Wister. I tried reading it about the time I was in fifth grade but the writing was too frosty for me. The trouble was, as I realized when I tried again thirty or so years later, that Owen Wister was a very proper late-nineteenth-century Philadelphian and wrote like one much of the time. Left to his own devices, his narrator is liable to spill out sentences like these in the first chapter: "Have you ever seen a cockatoo—the white kind with the top-knot—enraged by insult? The bird erects every available feather upon its person. So did Uncle Hughey seem to swell, clothes, mustache, and woolly white beard; and without further speech he took himself on board the East-bound train, which now arrived from its siding in time to deliver him. . . . With him now the East-bound departed slowly into that distance whence I had come. I stared after it as it went its way to the far shores of civilization."[7] That's a lighthearted, joking passage; I will forebear quoting from one of the descriptions of the solemn beauty of the mountains.

Perhaps because his own natural language is so stiffly genteel—and because he did have enough sense to notice that Mark Twain had been at work in recent decades—Wister was fascinated with the speech of the cowhands his narrator talked with. He tried valiantly to reproduce their pronunciation and failed; but he succeeded in catching a lot of the syntactical elisions that characterize Western speech as well as its deadpan ways with diction. Thus in the second chapter he got his great line. Well, he almost got it. He muddied the context because he could not actually quote profanity and coyly noted that the cowhands were using "son-of-a - ———" in a surprising variety of ways. When the bad guy says across the poker table, "Your bet, you son-of-a- ———," the hero replies

7. Owen Wister, *The Virginian*, 7.

softly, even gently, "When you call me that, *smile!*"[8] The movie's version is better. Wister's version is a direct order, and it is backed up by a pistol on the table. In the movie, Coop does not have to display his gun, and he does not so much give an order as make a suggestion, "Smile when you say that, pardner." That friendly word "pardner" at the end of the suggestion is every bit as ominous as Coop's tight-eyed look when he says it. The force of the statement lies in what it does not say in so many words; it lies in the difference between the denotation of "partner"—its significance as a sign—and its connotation—its significance as a symbol—in this particular context. This is first-class talk.

It's plain enough what Wister admired about his hero. His narrator, who is like himself a visitor from the very proper if not downright effete East, describes the Virginian, who is very much a man of the West even though he comes originally from Virginia, as "a slim young giant, more beautiful than pictures," dust covered from many miles of riding on the plains. Yet he is so much more attractive than Uncle Hughey, who has been "swept and garnished" for his wedding, that, as the narrator says, "had I been the bride, I should have taken the giant, dust and all."[9] Something akin to that sexual envy seems involved in Wister's admiration of the western way of talking. He stresses its freedom from the elaborate codes of manners and of social deference that constrict genteel speech, its openness to banter and playfulness and to gesture and intonation as a means of qualifying meaning. Though the men he admired were not in the least vulgar or promiscuous (the twentieth century was just beginning and Wister really was a proper Philadelphian) they were *men*, fully capable of maintaining their own freedom in speech and in action, who would, if need be, tell anyone talking carelessly anywhere to smile if they're going to say things like that.

I do not argue that Americans actually are freer than other people (the twentieth century is about over and I do not need my head examined). We are related to Wister's bad guy, Trampas, as well as to the Virginian; most of us have had to learn something about smiling whether we feel like it or not, and some of us have

8. Ibid., 29.
9. Ibid., 4–5.

gotten too good at it for comfort. Still, when we get to talking to ourselves and to people we think we can trust, we can't help talking as though we were free to say what we want to say. That implication seems to be built into the idioms and the rhythms given to us to use; even our glummest determinists, our behavioral psychologists and Marxists, can't help but talk as though they were the ones who decided what they should say. Even our deconstructionists write as though they are not liable to deconstruction themselves. I do not know precisely where and when it all started; I hope that a Pilgrim one step west of Plymouth Rock put an American twist on a sentence in recognition of the truth that people willing to take chances with their lives are free to take chances with their language. If that is too much to hope for, I can certainly take as our symbolic starting point that moment in Philadelphia in 1776 when Benjamin Franklin told the leaders of the thirteen colonies, who had met to consider a Declaration of Independence, that "we must all hang together, or most assuredly we shall all hang separately." That is pure American.

Songs, movies, and speeches are all well and good, but my argument must deal with American writing, especially with the talk-filled prose of American fiction. *Talk-filled* is not simply the clumsy substitute for *vernacular* that it might seem to be. It serves as a recurring reminder of Walker Percy's ideas about language; also, it is a broader and therefore less misleading term than *vernacular*. *Vernacular* is a more or less scientific, heavily Latinate term that comes to most of us from lexicographers and grammarians who want to label words, phrases, and structures as substandard, smacking of the sweaty masses rather than of the literary and cultural elite. The opening of *Huckleberry Finn* is commonly cited as, and is, a classic of nineteenth-century vernacular prose, a beautifully clear rendition of the diction and syntax of an uneducated boy of that time and place. But how about the opening sentences of "Old Times on the Mississippi," "Fenimore Cooper's Literary Offenses," and "The Mysterious Stranger"? "When I was a boy there was but one permanent ambition among my comrades in our village on the west bank of the Mississippi River." "It seems to me that it was far from right for the Professor of English Literature in Yale, the Professor of English Literature in Columbia, and Wilkie Collins to deliver opinions on Cooper's literature without having read some of it." "It was in 1590—winter. Austria was far away from the world, and asleep; it was still the Middle Ages in Austria and promised to remain so forever." None of them feature the low diction and fractured grammar of Huck's great narrative, yet all of them are redolent of the diction and rhythms of American talk. No one but a specialist would classify them as *vernacular*. Save for a few occasions when his arteries got clogged with philosophical thoughts or genteel emotions, Twain seems to have been miraculously incapable of sounding like a writer rather than a talker. Similarly, *vernacular* does not seem a satisfactory label for or classification of Thoreau's prose in *Walden*, where, as he said, he did not "propose to write an ode to dejection, but to brag as lustily as Chanticleer in the morning, standing on his roost, if only to wake my neighbors up." *Vernacular* just isn't the word for "propose to write an ode to dejection" or "Chanticleer in the morning" but anybody with ears who grew up in New England knows that is a Yankee talking. Abraham Lincoln was the other great mid-nineteenth-century master of American prose. Garry Wills, in his remarkable analysis of the Gettysburg Address, *Lincoln at Gettysburg*, argues that it worked several revolutions, beginning with one in prose style, for it anticipated the shift to vernacular rhythm that Mark Twain completed some years later. Wills proves his point, very carefully, but that is as close as anyone would care to come to describing the prose of Gettysburg and the Second Inaugural as "vernacular," though again, anyone who hears what he reads will recognize it as the pure American article. Henry James is yet another very important case in point. I don't think anyone has ever described his style as "vernacular," at least not with a straight face, yet it is plainly, even notoriously, a talk-based style. Witness all the discussion of how his sentences became even more elaborate, even more densely packed with parenthetical qualifications, after he took to dictating his novels to a secretary. I have never, thank heavens, known anyone who talked at all like James, yet he talks constantly to his reader. That is why even a fast reader has to slow down when dealing with James: you can't skim his paragraphs as though they were written; you have to read them as though they were spoken. The rules against moving your lips while reading are suspended when you're reading James. But once you get the hang of it, you know that you are reading talk of a rare, very high order. People who say that they can't stand to read James's prose are to be forgiven on the grounds that tin ears are probably a birth defect of sorts.

Comparing James to T. S. Eliot can be highly instructive. Eliot seems to have gone to London to escape the fate of being American and became as quickly as he could as English as he could in as many different ways as he could. James had no urge to escape being American; he settled in London because it gave him, abundantly, material suitable to his gifts and his themes; in particular it gave him a view of America and Americans against a backdrop of Europe and Europeans. Eliot's critical essays are written in fine upper-class English prose; James's essays are in the often startlingly mannered prose that characterizes our peculiarly intense writers in the tradition that stretches from Melville to Mailer. Denis Donoghue makes a most important point in *Ferocious Alphabets* when he compares James and Eliot in the course of a discussion of Eliot's plays. "Henry James was more successful than Eliot in arranging relations between his super-subtle fry and his fools, mainly because fiction does not require, as drama does, the presentation of sharply distinguished levels and roles; and James was remarkably gifted in showing what Eliot could not bring himself to concede: that everyone is in some respects a fool."[10]

I think you can broaden that. I think that *all* of our major writers whose styles are obviously grounded in the language of American talk cheerfully concede with James that everyone really is in some respects a fool—Emerson, Thoreau, Melville, Whitman, Twain, Emily Dickinson, Frost, Mencken, William Carlos Williams, Hemingway, Faulkner, Eudora Welty, Henry Miller, Flannery O'Connor, Norman Mailer, and E. Annie Proulx will do for starters. That creates the suspicion—I'd call it a near certainty—that there is something about the language of American talk that tends to force us to admit our own foolishness. That may simply be a product of our highly publicized deference to the ideal of equality, but I think it is something more potent, and much more mysterious, than that. Whatever the cause, people who are good at handling that language admit their own foolishness; people who dare not admit that

10. Denis Donoghue, *Ferocious Alphabets*, 36–37.

they, too, are in some respect fools—pedants, bureaucrats, and Very Important Persons—handle the language of talk clumsily, if at all.

One last point, an indisputable one this time. American talk does not take kindly to abstractions and therefore is not a language for ideologues and ideologies. You can't smile when you say the things that true believers have to say: the Truth of True Believers does not admit to qualification, and the jargon in which they say it does not even so much as recognize the possibility of joking. A smile might crack the edifice of their Theory; a giggle could bring it down. That explains why so many of the followers of Ferdinand de Saussure are such painfully dull writers. It also explains why ideologues tend to dislike and distrust the masters of the language of American talk; for ideological purposes they are too dangerous. Our current group of dealers in critical theories is so distrustful of the language and of the shifty writers who have mastered it that they have developed the preposterous notion that the best writing for students to study is the writing of critical theorists. I used to think I was lucky to be able to read Hemingway and Faulkner, now I should feel sorry for them because they didn't get a chance to read me? I conclude that we should thank the Lord for all that jazzy, idiosyncratic, foolish, talk-filled American writing that is so busy being free that it cannot spare the time to accommodate an ideology, and I trust that there are people all over the world who would join us in doing so.

I am deeply aware of how lucky I was when my grandmother took me by the hand to the Park Theater one afternoon and I heard that magical line, "Smile when you say that, pardner." I was even luckier the day a few years later when I discovered among the books piled on my bed to keep me occupied while I recuperated from my annual bout of tonsillitis *Tom Sawyer* and *Huckleberry Finn.* I wish I could remember the names of all the books and all the writers who taught me to read with my ears; I would like to celebrate them one by one in gratitude for the pleasure I have had in hearing how the way of saying something can qualify the meaning of what is being written. But I have neither memory enough nor space enough to complete that catalog. They came in all sizes and shapes, so to speak. Some were as widely known as Ernest Hemingway; others were as obscure, at least at that time, as the sportswriter who wrote a column for the *Philadelphia Evening Record* named Red

Smith. They all did things for me, so by the time I left high school and went into the navy I was fully equipped with big ears, a big mouth, and the sense to distrust anybody who spoke the language of those who know better and expect to be admired for it. Such equipment was highly useful in 1943, not to mention the many years since.

2

The Matter of the Mind

Percy's tetradic theory of language has the charming effect of making it clear why I and nearly everyone else I know who delights in reading and struggles to write well hold the attitudes we do towards language. Though we are sometimes gushed over as "lovers of language" and more frequently sneered at as "snobs" or—worst of all—as "school marms," we are simply doing our best to meet the demands of the two lines of force that Percy identifies in his diagram. The horizontal line running between "symbol" and "object" that is labeled "Relation of Quasi-Identity" requires us, we think, to be greatly concerned with the history and denotation of a word or phrase and prone to debate with ourselves and with others the question of just what "objects" it may refer to. The vertical line running between "Organism 1" and "Organism 2" that is labeled "Relationship of Intersubjectivity" requires us to worry about the tone or connotation of a word or phrase and particularly about how the persons we're speaking or writing to will take that term—does it strike them the same way it strikes us? Language fascinates us and we don't care (we really don't) what the hustlers of linguistics say about how old-fashioned and undemocratic we are. We know—because Mark Twain told us so—that "the difference between the right word and the almost right word is the difference between the lightning and the lightning bug" and we know—because our mothers told us so—that we should be careful of the company we keep. Fashion has nothing to do with the need for and delight in accuracy, and the ideals of democracy have very little to do with the desire to speak and write in the language used by people whose judgment we respect. I know, for example, that the verb *to enthuse* is used by so many people that no lexicographer would think of condemning it, but since no writer that I admire will use it, the word has never crossed my tongue or my word processor. I will cheerfully split infinitives because I think that most good writers do, and like them, much of the time I would rather use an "ungrammatical" *who* than a stuffily correct *whom*. In these matters I may be idiosyncratic and I know that others in my clan would give other examples. The point is that the matters of grammar and syntax that linguists exercise so much logic upon tend to bore us; we follow our ears into the endlessly fascinating matters of semantics and tone.

I regret to say that though a lot of my friends have read Percy's novels with enthusiasm I doubt that very many of them have read *The Message in the Bottle,* partly because they tend to recoil from terms like *tetradic diagrams,* but mostly because they rarely find much nourishment in philosophical speculations about language or in analytical disquisitions on grammar and syntax. No harm done—they already know that language is talk. The failure of the professionals in departments of philosophy and linguistics to pay attention to Percy's book is a much more serious matter. Steven Pinker, Director of the Center for Cognitive Neuroscience at the Massachusetts Institute of Technology, is a startlingly clear case in point. His defensive celebration of Chomskyan linguistics, *The Language Instinct: How the Mind Creates Language,* worked well enough with reviewers who hadn't read Percy that the publishers of the paperback edition were able to gather six pages of glowing praise from semi-august and even downright-august sources, but anyone who comes to it from a reading of *The Message in the Bottle* will be struck by how badly Pinker needs to learn things Percy could readily teach him—or perhaps I should say by how feeble his argument is in places because he hasn't been willing to learn such lessons.

Not having anything approaching an understanding of the nature of a symbol and its "relationship of quasi-identity" with its referent, Pinker thinks that *symbol* means the same thing as *sign* and will use either term in discussing the function of words. Early in his chapter "How Language Works," he picks up on Saussure's phrase "the arbitrariness of the sign," which he interprets as "the wholly conventional pairing of a sound with a meaning. The word *dog* does not look like a dog, walk like a dog, or woof like a dog, but it means 'dog' just the same. It does so because every English speaker has undergone an identical act of rote learning in childhood that links the sound to the meaning. For the price of this standardized memorization, the members of a language community receive an enormous benefit: the ability to convey a concept from mind to mind virtually instantaneously."[1] Pinker doesn't bother to remember that first a child has experience with several quite different looking animals named "Prince" and "Muggs" and "Chips" and so forth, and only then manages the piece of synthesizing (not "rote") learning that all of them and a lot of other animals more or less like them are called "dogs." Nor does he pause to realize that there may be some surprising differences in the concept that gets from one mind to another at the mention of the word *dog*. Given all of those possible differences, *dog* is much more a symbol than a sign, or if it is a sign it is an exceedingly abstract one. Certainly there is nothing approaching a tidy one-to-one relationship between the word "dog" and whatever it is referring to at the moment—a pet, a pest, a class of animals, an unattractive woman, or an energetically lustful man. Percy is right; what we have here is at best a relationship of *quasi-identity*. Pinker, like most other linguists, pays much too little attention to semantics in formulating his theory of "how language works" to give thought to subtleties of identification.

A more serious flaw in his argument is his nearly total failure to realize that language is a social construct, neither developed by nor possessed by one person alone. He argues, as Chomsky does, that "children must innately be equipped with a plan common to the grammars of all languages, a Universal Grammar, that tells them how to distill the syntactic patterns out of the speech of their parents." A few chapters later he explains further that "each person's brain contains a lexicon of words and the concepts they stand for (a mental dictionary) and a set of rules that combine the words to convey relationships among concepts (a mental grammar)." Since he is out to argue that language is an innate capacity, an inherited "instinct," that notion of a mental dictionary has to be qualified, for how can a French child inherit a French lexicon and an English-speaking child an English lexicon? He attempts to solve the problem by postulating a universal language, "mentalese," that everyone possesses as birthright and subsequently learns to translate into

1. Steven Pinker, *The Language Instinct: How the Mind Creates Language*, 83–84.

French or English or whatever. As solutions to problems go, that one doesn't go very far. But he is so anxious to make language strictly a matter between an individual and evolution that he dare not admit that it is in any significant way something a child learns from others. He doesn't comment on Helen Keller, being too much a social scientist and too little a novelist to stoop to particular cases, but apparently he would have us believe that even in the prison of her deaf-muteness the poor child was fluent in "mentalese" and that Miss Sullivan merely helped her with some problems of translation. When he does pause to consider talk he renders it a one-way transaction, like an academic lecture, marveling at the ability "to dispatch an infinite number of precisely structured thoughts from head to head by modulating exhaled breath."[2] I don't think that the word "communication" occurs in Pinker's nearly five hundred pages; I am quite certain that its companion term "communion" does not.

In short, I think that *The Language Instinct* is a bad book that uses a debater's flimflam tricks to persuade us that Chomskyan linguistics is grounded in evolutionary certainties and that we therefore have no choice but to embrace its major conclusions. Even a quick comparison with Walker Percy's essays is enough to reveal the radical faults in Pinker's argument—and in Chomsky's ideas, too—but it's hard to persuade people to give the heave to a theory that everyone has heard so much about. That's the trouble. Everyone has heard about it, but few have ever read Chomsky or thought carefully about the implications of his ideas. I suspect that most people have been intimidated by the Chomskyans' scornful analyses of the old-fashioned Latin-based grammar. True, English is not a Latin language. True, in a lot of important ways the Latin-based grammar simply doesn't make good sense. But it is also true that long before the Chomskyans came on the scene everybody knew that English is a Germanic, not a Latinate language, and nearly everybody had noticed that the grammar they had been taught in school was full of holes. Still, "the grammar of the schoolmarms" made a dandy straw man for the Chomskyans to beat. They are still pounding on it— Pinker devotes his next to last chapter to mocking it for its prescriptive ways. This is foolishness; we do not have to swallow a

2. Ibid., 22, 85, 362.

Chomskyan grammar (commonly called "transformational grammar") just because a Latinate grammar is faulty. Language is not a simple either-or proposition.

For a far better understanding of how language evolved and of how the mind deploys it, as well as for an even more devastating critique of Chomsky's ideas, we have to turn from the social sciences to the physical and biological sciences, which is for most humanists a turn from the moderately familiar though somewhat awkward to the strange and intimidating. I cheerfully admit that I am about to get in way over my head. Before I stumbled into the need to know something about how the brain really does work with respect to language, I knew close to nothing about neurology, brain structure, amines, cholines, algorithms, and quantum mechanics. But I discovered there are a number of top-flight scientists who are anxious to report the results of the work they and their peers have been doing in such a way that a humanist can, with a little patient effort, follow their arguments. Though I still have no expertise (to put it very mildly) in neurology, biology, chemistry, physics, and so forth, I have learned from these scientists enough to understand the implications their work has for the humanities. Indeed, I have come to the quite unexpected conclusion that although it is easier for us to understand the ideas of social scientists, because they finally get expressed in words, than it is to follow physical and biological scientists through their thickets of mathematics, we are in one hugely important intellectual respect closer to the physical scientists: we are both accustomed to working with a large number of specific facts before placing much trust in our ideas. The social scientists appear to begin by formulating generalized concepts and then searching for data that will support them. This description may not be fair, but certainly the discourse of social scientists seems painfully abstract to anybody who has spent his life happily wading in works of literature. The discourse of physical scientists may be abstruse but it is not abstract. The habits of fashionable Theorists notwithstanding, critics who can not marshal evidence in support of their arguments are worthless; so, too, are scientists who do not know what constitutes adequate evidence for their propositions. One other observation: humanists and physical scientists can freely acknowledge the role that luck and hunches play in even their best work; social scientists are liable to turn haughty at any suggestion that luck has affected their performance in gathering and analyzing data. That may seem to be a trivial distinction but it is not. It's the difference between people who know they are dealing ultimately with mystery and people who think they are dealing with problems that will yield to a rigorously rational analysis.

(In *This Is Biology*, a remarkable book that manages to be interesting and instructive both to the experienced scientists who have reviewed it and to humanists like myself who haven't seen the inside of a laboratory since their sophomore year in college, Ernst Mayr asserts that "literary criticism has virtually nothing in common with most of the other disciplines of the humanities and even less with science."[3] I think that Mayr has, understandably enough, let his exasperation with the postmodernist peddlers of theory, who assume that they know everything worth knowing about anything they stoop to discussing, get the better of him; actually, literary criticism as it is practiced by old-fashioned, or resolutely unfashionable, scholars and critics who marshal evidence and hope for luck has significant similarities to the science Mayr himself practices. The biological sciences, he insists, are radically different from the physical sciences because they deal with living organisms rather than with the inanimate world and therefore must constantly deal with the duality arising from the fact that organisms possess both a genotype and a phenotype. Understanding the genotype, which is expressed in nucleic acids and is controlled by the genes, requires evolutionary, historical explanations; understanding the phenotype, which consists of proteins, lipids, and other macromolecules and is constructed on the basis of information provided by the genotype, requires functional explanations. To put it in less technical terms, biology deals with living organisms, and any understanding of their nature requires explanation in terms of both their historical or evolutionary and their proximate or functional causes. Only dual explanations are adequate, for an organism always has both a historical and an ahistorical dimension; any singular explanation must, of necessity, be false. Well, literature, which is one of the distinguishing works of the human organism, requires a very similar kind of duality of explanation. Roughly speaking, a given work of literature takes its form from the history of other works and

3. Ernst Mayr, *This Is Biology*, 37.

its content from the experience of its writer; a novel, poem, or play is as it is because it finds its place at the end of a sequence of many other novels, poems, and plays and because it comes out of the life of the person who wrote it. Only fools and ideologues think that literature yields to singular explanations.)

I want to begin by taking a careful look at *Bright Air, Brilliant Fire: On the Matter of the Mind* by Gerald M. Edelman. Edelman is a scientist of impressive accomplishments. Edelman won the Nobel Prize in 1972 for his studies of the immune system and went on from there to develop a theory of how the mind and the nervous system work that led to the publication between 1987 and 1990 of a monumental trilogy describing his research and his "Theory of Neuronal Group Selection" for the benefit of his fellow specialists in the neurosciences. In 1994 he presented his resolutely Darwinian theory informally and with wide-ranging historical and philosophical discussion in *Bright Air, Brilliant Fire*, thereby making it accessible to nonspecialists—at least to those who don't mind having to do some careful reading and thinking about unfamiliar subjects. Anybody who takes language and literature seriously should be willing to make the effort, for the book has important implications affecting every aspect of the work we do. Certainly it speaks very strongly to the issues I have been discussing thus far.

Edelman is not out to reform the humanities in general and literary criticism in particular; he is a biologist with a biologist's concern to develop an appropriately deep and rigorous understanding of how the processes of evolution worked on the brain to produce the conscious mind. However, he does deal specifically with Chomsky's theory of language, which he rejects; and he comments briefly but favorably on Percy's "Martian" ideas. (Unlike Steven Pinker he has read *The Message in the Bottle*.) More importantly, he makes a number of assertions on matters of obvious importance to humanists and supports those assertions with a great deal of persuasive evidence: Human consciousness is the product of the evolutionary development of the human brain; the processes of the brain are organic and nothing like the processes of computers; objectivist theories of language such as Chomsky's and Saussure's are flatly wrong; physical realities are problematic rather than determined; no two human beings are identical in their physical structure, their history, or their minds; and a command of figures of speech and of narrative are essential for the operation of the mind. If Edelman is not only right but can go a very long way towards *demonstrating* he's right about these and other matters, then humanists would be exceedingly well advised to pay attention to him.

Begin with some numbers. Ten billion—that's a reasonable estimate of the number of neurons in the cerebral cortex, the part of the brain that deals with higher brain functions such as speech, thought, complex movement patterns, and music. One million billion—that's the number of synapses, or connections, among those neurons. As amazing as those numbers are, Edelman thinks that an even more remarkable property of the brain is the way in which the cells, each of which possesses numerous synapses, are arranged in functioning patterns. "When this exquisite arrangement of cells (their microanatomy, or morphology) is taken together with the number of cells in an object the size of your brain, and when one considers the chemical reactions going on inside, one is talking about the most complicated material object in the known universe."[4]

The mere numbers alone are nearly enough to make me accept the proposition that the brain is an organism capable of generating the qualities of a mind and further that it is totally unlike anything so puny as a computer. Computers are the electronic kin of mechanisms, cousins in the family of manufactured devices, and are designed by human beings to be both effective and efficient; as a rule, the simpler their parts and the more direct their connections the better. This "most complicated material object in the known universe" is an organism working in organic ways. Organisms seek profusion, developing a multiplicity of pathways and possibilities; the more ways of functioning and of surviving the better. Pull a single part at random from any well-designed mechanism and its operation will probably be impaired, possibly even stopped; take a leaf, a branch, or even a major limb from a tree and it will keep on functioning. A strong surge in electrical power will make junk of electronic gear; a bolt of lightning may or may not kill a tree. No mechanism can "afford" billions more connective points than it "needs" to have; an organism generates synapses in profusion so that it will always have plenty of different ways of getting a neural

---

4. Gerald M. Edelman, *Bright Air, Brilliant Fire: On the Matter of the Mind*, 17.

impulse from one place to another. In the presence of the brain's astronomical numbers of neurons and synapses it becomes difficult to believe that a computer can ever do more than simulate a small part of the brain's activities. Computer makers have done ingenious things to circumvent these limitations, but no matter how flashy their programming and how brilliant their designing, they are still operating in a mechanistic, not an organic, system. To put it all another way, those billions upon billions of cells and synapses are the brain's "hardware"; its "software" is simply beyond description. The hardware parts of a computer do not come by the billions, but even if they did its software can be described exactly, for it is the handiwork of human programmers. I have to think that the amount of intelligence that can be created artificially will remain very small indeed.

Edelman does not trifle with chitchat of that exclamatory sort. He shows through careful, lucid argument that is well buttressed with evidence just how the human brain could and did evolve so as to produce a conscious mind. I can manage only the roughest sort of sketch of that subtle, fascinating argument.

I would begin by stressing his distinction between systems of instruction and systems of selection. Computers work by instructions: if this, then that. Powerful computers programmed by very capable programmers can do remarkably subtle things, but finally nothing can happen in an instructional system, not even, I think, one that exploits the latest schemes for randomization, that has not been in some way anticipated and allowed for. Evolution works by selection: possibilities arise by genetic accidents in a population of organisms, creating variations from the norm. If a given variation increases the chances of survival for the individual organisms possessing it then they and their descendants will flourish and the strains lacking that genetic variation will gradually get crowded out. The possibilities for variation are endless and therefore beyond the reach of anticipation. That is to say, a system of selection from among the possibilities presented by accidental variations will always be richer than a system of instruction, which is necessarily limited by the nature of the instruction; over time it will always be far more powerful, too. Many humanists, many people of all sorts, resist that Darwinian idea; it sounds too messy, too irrational to be right, and rather demeaning to boot. Yet it isn't demeaning, not really; the thought that we came to be what we are by means of a long, slow, irresistible process of change and growth is finally most comforting. ("My foothold is tenon'd and mortise'd in granite," sang Walt Whitman, "I laugh at what you call dissolution, and I know the amplitude of time.") But like it or not, the inescapable truth is that the brain, like the rest of the body, has evolved by a system of selection and it employs, as the rest of the body does, systems of selection.

Evolution requires large amounts of time to work; our internal systems of selection apparently require those astronomical cellular resources to work. Having such an abundance of resources the brain could evolve what might seem to be a profligate way of working that employs patterned clusters of cells and synapses to deal with each part of a task. For example, the brain divides the process of seeing over several different clusters or "maps," a fact that has been demonstrated in experiments with animals with comparatively simple brain structures. The rays of light that fall on the various parts of the retina in an animal's eye set off electrical signals that are registered in a cluster in the animal's brain in such a fashion as to map the location of the original stimuli on the retina, but those signals have an unpredictable number of ways of getting to the map and are received by not one but a number of different maps simultaneously. Each map specializes in dealing with a different aspect of the retinal image, and each is connected with the other retinal maps as well as with nonretinal maps by means of overlapping and branching "arbors" of fibers. Seeing, then, is the product of a synthesis of what is registered on a number of different maps at once, some of them dealing with retinal events and some dealing with such very different matters as similar previous experiences and survival values. It was not enough for that bird of Emily Dickinson's that came hopping down the walk to see a slithery brownish elongation; it had to compare that experience with earlier experiences with things that turned out to be worms on the walk and that were good to eat. Only then could it bite the fellow in half and eat him, raw. I could not even begin to guess at all of the maps, or neuronal groups, in Emily Dickinson's brain that led her to go on to describe the bird as unrolling his feathers and rowing him softer home than oars divide an ocean too silver for a seam.

The example is mine, but following Edelman I would say that

two kinds of consciousness are represented in the poem: the bird's, "primary consciousness," and the poet's, "higher-order consciousness." I am, I repeat, going to have to proceed quite roughly; I cannot do justice to Edelman's careful but highly compressed account of the neuroscientific bases for the distinction. But let me first emphasize the obvious truth that some such distinction is there to be made. Plainly a great many animals have some kind of consciousness; just as plainly human beings have an additional, much more subtle and far-reaching kind of consciousness. One would think that it would be the job of those studying the mind to make that distinction fairly early on in their work; the ridiculous truth is that a great many of them have refused to have anything whatsoever to do with consciousness on the grounds that it is a subjective, therefore a nonverifiable, therefore a nonscientific phenomenon. The behavioral psychologists, for example, have spent years pretending that there is no such thing as consciousness, only behavior, which they can observe, measure, quantify, compare, chart, and so on.

Primary consciousness came first. It depends on the workings of the most fundamental parts of the nervous system, on the most primitive part of the brain, which is the brain stem, and on the simplest, earliest to evolve capacities of the cortex. Primary consciousness serves the animal's most basic needs, the appetites, and its defensive, fight-or-flight systems. Acting something like a flashlight in a dark room, primary consciousness enables the animal to make a "scene" out of what is before it and therefore to know what to do with or about what it sees and thereby greatly enhances the animal's ability to survive. To put the matter technically, primary consciousness correlates signals from the two major subsystems of the overall nervous system—the system of the interior that governs all of the body's involuntary functions and its nearly involuntary responses, and the thalamocortical system that registers signals about exterior happenings and categorizes them. The interior, or limbic-brain-stem, system maintains and enforces the self-centered "values" (nourishment, sleep, sexual satisfaction, etc.) and categorizes signals of events according to the values; the system of the exterior registers and categorizes the signals it receives about the world outside the self. When the two systems became linked so that the categorization of perception became responsive to the evolutionarily selected values, the way was open to increased powers of learning, then to the possibility of conceptual as well as perceptual categorization, and then just beyond that to primary consciousness, which is a complex knowledge of the present moment.

If all that is too much to swallow at once, as well it might be, then let's just say that Edelman explains that the brain evolved towards consciousness in the way in which you might expect it to. First came a fairly simple sort of consciousness in which some awareness of what is going on inside the animal is connected with some awareness of what is going on outside with the result of gaining a considerable evolutionary advantage. Most animals developed that primary consciousness and stopped there. The human animal went one enormous step farther; while still retaining the powers of primary consciousness, it acquired language and with it large powers of symbolic memory. That is to say, *Homo erectus* very quickly (as such things go in evolution) became *Homo sapiens*, the talking animal who is fully conscious of being conscious, who knows that the world and the self have been, are, and always will be two very different matters.

Let me go back to square one. The human brain did evolve over time, becoming much larger and much more complicated. A surprisingly detailed history of that evolution can be reconstructed by studies of fossils and by anatomical studies of existing animals. Edelman's statements about the evolutionary sequence can be taken as very well established. His statements about the functions of the evolving parts seem to be equally valid. His explanations of how the various parts are able to do the things he says they do are perhaps a little more theoretical, and possibly other neuroscientists might want to quarrel with one detail or another of his Theory of Neuronal Group Selection. But he has tested it through many series of well-devised experiments, and it is on the whole so coherent and so convincing that most of his scientific peers have accepted it. (See, for example, the "Special Report on Mind and Brain" *Scientific American* published in 1994 and the news reports of the White House Symposium on Early Childhood Development held on April 17, 1997.) I think that for our purposes we humanists can safely treat it as proven.

When you come at the problem cold, it is almost impossible to believe that a material object, the brain, could develop such immaterial capacities as the ability to think and to make metaphors and the power to be conscious of the self being conscious; but by the time Edelman has taken you through the development bit by bit it is easy to believe that having evolved a rudimentary capacity to categorize perceptions by means of concepts the brain would finally evolve a system of representing concepts abstractly, language. Anyway, if you try to deny that matter can generate spirit, as many philosophers have in the past, you are stuck with an absolute impossibility: the necessity to postulate a little homunculus tucked inside the brain telling it what to make of the images it is receiving and then to postulate a still smaller homunculus inside the first one, and so on in an infinite regression. Though at first glance it seems easier and more attractive to believe that the mind works by some system of instruction for dealing with reality, it is finally simpler and more satisfying to acknowledge that the mind, like the brain, operates by a system of selection, taking from the welter of circumstances surrounding it bits of impression that it can arrange in its own way to make its own kind of sense of what is out there.

To come back for a moment to the well-publicized dream of artificial intelligence, minds are capable of intelligence, consciousness, self-awareness, social interaction, and so forth because they are embodied; computers are not. The programmed resources of hardware and software seem paltry in comparison with the improvisational subtlety and power of a living body. Computers can only compute what and how they are instructed to compute; embodied minds can compute, dream, argue, embellish, summarize, ignore, falsify, and translate. Minds can experience emotions and fuse them with thoughts; they can either forget or remember, as they wish.

Despite his insistence that the brain is nothing like a computer, and despite his skeptical view of conventional schemes of artificial intelligence, Edelman does believe that it might be possible in the future to construct what he terms an "artifact"—a machine that makes some use of but is not itself a computer—that possesses primary consciousness. If that were to happen, he thinks it conceivable, though by no means likely, that an artifact possessing higher-order consciousness could be constructed. He himself has been working with machines that simulate the working of maps and loops in some of the brain's simpler structures; indeed, he has already used such a device in his laboratory to confirm aspects of his Theory of Neuronal Group Selection. His latest artifact is capable of "learning," in the biological sense of the word. Its functions are crude and simple by the standards of any living animal; but even so a supercomputer is necessary to operate it. For Edelman, though computers are powerful tools for the exploration of neuroscientific problems, they are only tools, not models.

If minds are embodied, so is language. Language is the great, distinguishing, powerful, fascinating attribute-accomplishment of the embodied mind. It could not come into being until evolution had created certain structures in the brains and bodies of our precursors and it had to have grown out of the development of certain powers in primary consciousness—crucially, the ability to formulate and remember simple concepts relating perceptions to the basic values for survival. Language thus began with semantics, relating phonological symbols, words, to concepts. After a sufficiently large lexicon was collected and put to use in primitive kinds of speech the conceptual areas of the brain would have categorized the *order* of speech elements and then stabilized it in memory as syntax. The point is important. Semantics preceded syntax. The brain acts selectively, not by instruction. It must have recursively related semantic to phonological sequences and then have generated syntactic correspondences, "not from preexisting rules, but by treating rules *developing in memory* as objects of conceptual manipulation."[5]

This is an entirely different view of the evolution of language from Steven Pinker's; it is also much more persuasive. Edelman rejects Pinker's and Chomsky's theory of language because it assumes that syntax precedes semantics and holds that some universal syntactical scheme at the root of all languages is inborn in all humans and constitutes a language faculty that is quite unlike and essentially independent of other cognitive capabilities. That simply doesn't fit with everything else that Edelman knows about the mind and about language; in fact, it doesn't fit with any part of the growing body of knowledge about how the mind works. Edelman dismisses it as unscientific because it can be neither proved nor disproved by referring to facts about cognition in general and because it has failed to generate any further scientifically valid hypotheses about language. I think we have to chalk up Chomsky's grammar simply as an inspired hunch that awakened old-fashioned

5. Ibid., 130.

philologians from their Latinate dreams and forced newer-fashioned linguists to think about how human beings acquire, develop, and use language. For an answer to the question of how a child can master the complexities of language, Chomsky can't do better than a half-joking proposal of a "language acquisition device" in the child's brain; that comes uncomfortably close to postulating a little black box of the sort beloved by bad science fiction writers. Infants don't need little black boxes; they listen to their parents, grandparents, and siblings talk to and around them. As Edelman has shown, they are, like the first *Homo sapiens*, highly evolved creatures who have ample neurological resources for juggling words until they yield syntactical patterns so that the children can take their places in the language communities to which they belong.

Saussure's theories go down the drain with Chomsky's, if only because, as Colin Falck demonstrates, they treat language as disembodied, ignoring the fact that it could only have arisen from an experience with meaningful bodily gestures that has been shared with other persons. "The categories of Saussurian theory . . . cannot avoid misrepresenting or belying the true nature of conceptual language and of the relationship in which it stands to the world we live in." Saussure's followers among postmodernist theorists have grossly amplified the effect of his treatment of language as disembodied and have thereby managed to conclude that language can never be finally meaningful. They complain of ambiguity and seem to think that language should yield to a true-false test. It does not, both Edelman and Falck would have us insist, because it does not exist between a world and an observer, it exists among a group of people who want and need to tell each other about their experiences and their feelings in all their ambiguous richness. Edelman cites with approval Percy's argument that "all symbolic exchanges involving meaning show a tetradic relationship between symbol, object, and at least two human beings." He relishes Percy's "dense and resonant" statement that "the act of consciousness is the intending of the object as being what it is for both of us under the auspices of a symbol."[6]

Edelman's vision of the embodied mind with its insistence on the power (and, I think, the beauty, too) of systems that work by

6. Falck, *Myth*, 17; Edelman, *Bright Air*, 245.

selection rather than by instruction is hard on all of the theories and ideologies that have been popular in the intellectual marketplace in recent decades. Life happens in time, and over time variation, change, and individuality prevail everywhere. To put it another way, the macroscopic world we experience is full of things bearing a sort of family (or slight or fleeting) resemblance to other things; neat resemblances showing clear if partial identities are the exception. Our minds, when we don't bedevil them with logic, are beautifully set up to make the most of those family resemblances, for all the way down to the bottom of our primary consciousness we will put things in the same category if they seem in any way like each other. We sort out those grab bags later, one way if we are trying to argue carefully, another way if we are writing lyrics or telling stories.

I don't see any way of avoiding the conclusion that all deterministic theories of human character and behavior are wrong—just as wrong as deterministic theories of subatomic behavior. We are a mass of probabilities, not certainties, though no Heisenberg has formulated an uncertainty principle to apply to us. The simple truth is that both inside and outside our bodies and brains, in both the microscopic and the macroscopic worlds, nothing can be determined until after it happens. That is not to say that anything goes. We operate within constraints, of course, but they are only constraints, not iron rails.

The fundamental transaction, so to speak, in the mind's work is the taking in of something new or newly occurring inside or outside the body, categorizing it in some way, placing it somehow in the context of earlier experience, and deciding what if anything to do about it. In other words, among the mind's most fundamental skills are an ability to manage comparisons and an ability to relate present to past perceptions and events. In still other words, the mind needs to know how to use and respond to figures of speech and how to tell and respond to stories. Logic and mathematics are lovely things for a mind to have some mastery of, but language, figures of speech, and story are the stuff with which the mind creates its sense of our selves and of our worlds.

Though his 1972 Nobel Prize was for work in "Physiology or Medicine," Edelman is entirely the physical scientist and his work on the brain is focused on the fundamental scientific issue of how the mind evolved as an aspect of matter and not at all on any primarily medical issues. J. Allan Hobson is very much a medical man—a professor of psychology at Harvard Medical School and director of the Laboratory of Neurophysiology at the Massachusetts Mental Health Center—and he is not so much concerned to explore how mind evolved from matter as to gain new insights for dealing with psychiatric illness by acting on a conviction that mind and matter are two aspects of the same thing. Yet I don't think there is any important disagreement between the two men. Hobson's book, *The Chemistry of Conscious States: How the Brain Changes Its Mind,* was published less than two years after *Bright Air, Brilliant Fire* and comports perfectly with it. I presume that the trilogy Edelman had published earlier for a scientific audience made Hobson well aware of the theory of neuronal group structures; certainly a knowledge of it makes *The Chemistry of Conscious States* easier to understand. Still, it is grounded in careful and copious research and has exceedingly important implications for literary criticism as well as for psychiatry (even though it suffers from the ministrations of two editors and a journalist who put a coat of Marin County varnish on Hobson's scientific prose).

Hobson's story, beginning with his work in the "sleep laboratory" at the Massachusetts Mental Health Center that led him to a deeper understanding of how the conscious mind works and reinforced his conviction that the mind and the brain are a single unified thing, pivots on two seemingly simple decisions. One was to investigate the form of dreams rather than their content (because he thinks analysis of content has proved to be a dead-end street); the other was to utilize an old-fashioned device, the mental status exam, a question-and-answer format that has long been used to reveal signs of organic disease of the brain, to analyze the significance of the forms dreams take. Thus when he considers the dream of a woman named Delia (one of the volunteer subjects in the lab) in which she found herself flying over Paris in a balloon with her father and two sisters, Hobson is not led into any speculations about the repressed sexual implications of dreaming of flying with her father; rather he is led to the quite certain conclusion that a dream about ballooning over a Paris where the dreamer could see both a little boy peeing in the North Sea and the Al-Aqsa Mosque with some twenty-eight buildings attached to it bears all the hallmarks of an organic mental syndrome, delirium. To state it more carefully, he concludes that "Delia's brain-mind dream state matches exactly the brain-mind waking state of someone who suffers from an organic mental syndrome."[7] Apparently whatever is turned on or off when a healthy person like Delia begins to dream is the same as whatever is turned on or off in the brain of one of Hobson's psychotic patients when, fully awake, he becomes convinced that airplanes are about to strafe the area and he dives under a parked car for protection. Hobson hopes that the dream state will become a mirror in which the processes that produce pathological psychosis can be seen.

Concentrating on the features of all dreams, not on the secrets that may or may not be revealed in particular dreams, he can also hope to learn a lot about how healthy brains cause minds to work. The features missing from dreams are at least as significant as the ones that recur in them. Chief among the missing are the higher-level mental activities and the large-scale actions of the voluntary muscles. In dreams no one, not even professors like Hobson, or like me, either reads or writes, nor does anyone actually pump his legs or swing his arms no matter how vividly the dream convinces him he is running or fending off attackers. But all dreamers try their best to impose some kind of order and coherence on the episodes of a dream. Plainly something happens in the dream state to cut off the various rational powers and the actions of the large muscles; plainly, too, even in the dream state we will strain to find a way to give plausibility to whatever actions we think we are involved in, no matter how implausible they might be. What cuts off reasoning and immobilizes the muscles this way? What are the implications of that powerful drive to create coherence and plausibility? What is the root cause of this wild dreaming? And what could possibly be the evolutionary function of such mental behavior? Scientifically sound answers to these and a lot of other questions have become possible only in recent years with the development of technology that makes possible the observation of events in the brain.

For quite a few years scientists have known that in sleeping for six to eight hours an individual will go through four or five cycles

---

7. J. Allan Hobson, *The Chemistry of Conscious States: How the Brain Changes Its Mind*, 44.

of sleep and that each cycle will contain four progressively deeper stages of sleep. Generally, a person descends through the stages fairly rapidly to reach stage four where all systems both within and without the brain slow down and no dreams occur. Then as the cycle moves towards its end the sleeper ascends through the third and second stages to reach the first, the lightest stage, where many systems become quite active, the eyes begin to dart back and forth behind the closed eyelids, and dreams occur. Those rapid eye movements are the well-known signature of dreaming, and stage one sleep is labeled REM sleep. (Scientists do love their acronyms.) In recent years Hobson and his associates have been able to study in depth the activities of the brain and the eye muscles during REM sleep. They have attached sensitive electrodes to volunteers sleeping in the laboratory and measured the movements of their eye muscles and the electrical activity in their brains; then they have correlated those measurements with measurements made when the volunteers were awake and looking about. Further, with the invention of devices for scanning electrical activity in the brain, they have been able to see just where the activity is occurring. Thus the scientists don't have to guess, they know that in REM sleep in physiological fact as well as in mental hallucination we are quite busy looking around. What the scans can do to make visible the electrical activity of the nerves involved with moving the eyes and seeing, they can also do for the electrical activity in all of the other parts of the brain. The days of guessing about what's going on in the brain and where appear to be coming to a close.

Hobson can see that in REM sleep the parts of the brain associated with reasoning and with the voluntary muscles are relatively quiescent and other parts that deal with emotions and with patterns of motor responses are quite active. Further, he knows as a result of other research that "when we are awake our brain-minds are in the grip of one chemical system, and when we are dreaming our brain-minds are in the grip of a completely different chemical system. When both systems are at half-throttle, we sleep deeply with no dreams and little or no mental activity."[8] The first is called the aminergic system because the molecules that do the work are amines; the second, the dreaming system, is called the cholinergic because its

8. Ibid., 14.

working molecule is acetylcholine. The effect of the amines is to facilitate the quickness of response and the sharpness of short-term memory that characterize wide-awake activity; the acetylcholines appear to weaken inhibitions while at the same time strengthening long-term memory. Under the influence of amines we are acutely conscious of what is going on around us and are capable of thinking rationally about it. Doused with acetylcholines, we are conscious only of the stories we fabricate at a mad rate to account for the signals buzzing around in our brains, but we can neither think reasonably about them nor remember what happened in them a very few minutes after waking up. In short, Hobson and his colleagues in sleep laboratories have surprisingly sharp, detailed knowledge of what goes on in the brain-mind in REM sleep. Their concern is with neurological science and psychiatry, but their discoveries have important implications for literary criticism.

First—most clearly and most emphatically—Hobson's findings destroy the validity of a Freudian interpretation of dreams, thereby knocking the props out from under Freudian interpretations of literature and making the whole ingenious business of "interpreting" the "hidden" meanings of literature seem less convincing than ever. Given the state of scientific knowledge of the operations of the brain in the first half of the twentieth century, the Freudian understanding of the operations of the mind in dreams had to be developed and expressed in highly abstract terms—the unconscious, wish-fulfillment, symbolic images, displacement, and so forth. Now that neuroscientists can closely observe and accurately measure the electrical events that characterize the operations of the brain, those abstractions won't do. Dreams don't well up from the unconscious—Hobson calls that term "an artificial construct"—they occur only during the REM stage of sleep and are provoked by electrical activity that originates in the part of the brain that governs automatic muscular activity and is closely associated with emotional responses. If the unconscious is an artificial construct and if the rational parts of the brain don't operate during REM sleep, then there is no more meaning in the content of a dream than in the content of a psychotic hallucination. But when those neurons fire in one part of the brain a "lower," nonrational part of the brain-mind responds as it always responds to the firing of neurons by trying to construct a story that will give at least a momentary coherence to what seems to be happening. That's a clumsy way of stating a very important point: whenever it is conscious of itself, the brain-mind creates a narrative ("confabulates" is Hobson's term) that attempts to account for, or at least give plausibility to, the sequence of events it seems to be involved in. The mind does not deal in symbols; it deals in associations that it uses to generate story lines. When we are awake, the story unfolding is the story of our lives and we relate *now* to *then* and sometimes to *soon*; when we are asleep, the unfolding story is an earnest, always futile attempt to gather from the ragbag of memory, usually though not always very recent memory, material for giving coherence to what we mistakenly think is going on. Dreams do not last long and our memory of them fades very rapidly after waking, unless, like Hobson's volunteers, we attempt to record them immediately and do so habitually. Freud and others thought that the dreams we have over the course of a single night are integral; but the evidence gathered from those volunteers in the sleep lab, who agree to be awakened each time the instruments show they have completed a dreaming sequence, gives no support to that belief.

A form of behavior as dramatic as REM sleep (which, incidentally, we share with cats and some other animals) must have adaptive, evolutionary value. Hobson's guess is that it serves to keep automatic motor-system programs ready to function and that it helps in the establishment of long-term memories. The neuronal firings, he thinks, are a checking out of the signals that command a response while the voluntary muscles are rendered inoperative; it is something like the way a mechanic checks an engine's spark plugs and timer while the transmission is disengaged. He also thinks that somehow while the dreaming is going on and the amines that generate short-term memories are largely suppressed, long-term memories get established. A lot of that account of dream states of mind may be speculative, but it makes evolutionary sense, as Freudian accounts do not, and it is certain that the brain-mind is one of the gaudier results of the evolution of our kind.

Since Hobson and Edelman both come out of the biological sciences and are evolutionists convinced of the validity of the Darwinian theory of evolution by selection, it may not be so surprising that they so strongly reinforce each other's major ideas and conclusions. If so, the reinforcement they receive from the work of a physicist and mathematician who has no special concern for Darwinian theories of evolution, Roger Penrose, may have special weight. Penrose has published two impressively speculative books, *The Emperor's New Mind* and *Shadows of the Mind*. The first concentrates on arguing against the so-called strong version of artificial intelligence that assumes brains operate like computers and concludes, therefore, that as computers increase in power they will come to possess consciousness. Very roughly speaking, Penrose challenges AI's basic assumptions with some highly sophisticated mathematical arguments that he manages to render clear even to a humanist with little math. *Shadows of the Mind* restates some of those mathematical arguments and elaborates on his convictions that the brain's most important activities take place on the level of quantum mechanics and that a full understanding of them awaits the development of a general theory bridging the gap between quantum and classical mechanics. The philosopher John Searle, who is not given to extravagant praise, says that *Shadows of the Mind* is the only book he knows "where you can find lengthy and clear explanations of two of the most important discoveries of the twentieth century, Gödel's incompleteness theorem and quantum mechanics."[9] Still, it is not an easy book to take in; most humanists will be grateful that Penrose has added a third book, *The Large, the Small, and the Human Mind*, that condenses and clarifies both of his main arguments.

The mathematical one that he develops in *The Emperor's New Mind* hinges on the concept of the algorithm. An algorithm can be roughly defined as a calculational procedure of some kind, such as the rules for doing division that we all learned in grade school and that most of us forgot after we got our first pocket calculator. The algorithm for dividing 400 by 16 is simple; the algorithm governing the complex procedures of the sort that computers routinely perform are much more complex but they can—indeed they must—be spelled out by computer programmers. All of the operations that computers perform are governed by the algorithms that programmers supply. Therefore, when proponents of strong AI predict that we will eventually have computers that are as intelligent, as fully conscious, even, as human beings, they are assuming that all of the functions of the brain are governed by sets of algorithms that can be

9. John R. Searle, "The Mystery of Consciousness, Part 1," 64.

duplicated by sufficiently skillful programmers and carried out by sufficiently powerful computers. Penrose shows that some important areas of mathematics lie outside the domain of algorithms. Though computers use algorithms to solve complicated problems quickly and accurately, they cannot establish the validity of the algorithms they use; the question of mathematical truth can be decided only by external means. Furthermore, there are some mathematical matters so complicated that algorithmic solutions would be too lengthy to be practical (even for a computer) as well as some that are noncomputable and therefore nonalgorithmic in their basic nature. I will spare myself the pain and embarrassment of trying to condense Penrose's patient, lucid demonstration of the logic involved and settle for bluntly stating two main points. One, Gödel's theorem states that any mathematical system broad enough to contain all the formulas of a formalized elementary number theory, any one whatever, must contain some statements that are neither provable nor disprovable by the means allowed within the system. Two, the square root of a negative number cannot be computed, but for a lot of purposes, especially in doing quantum physics, you have to deal with "complex" numbers that require the arbitrary assignment of a value to the square root of -1.

So much, I would think, for the possibility of AI. How can there be any room for arguing that any machine for making binary calculations can develop ideas so specifically beyond the reach of algorithmic calculations? Of course, a little matter like lack of room for an argument never stopped anybody from arguing; several issues of the electronic periodical *Psyche* were filled with valiant and—I think—unsuccessful attempts to refute his reasoning. (Do the AI people envision computers as stubbornly illogical, as comically pigheaded as human beings?) In *The Large, the Small, and the Human Brain,* Penrose adds a beautifully simple observation that seems to me to devastate the AI argument: "Gödel tells us that no system of computational rules can characterize the properties of the *natural numbers.* Despite the fact that there is no computational way of characterizing the natural numbers, any child knows what they are. All you do is to show the child different numbers of objects [such as a chart of drawings of circles, stars, and trees] and after a while they can abstract the notion of natural number from these particular instances of it. You do not give the child a set of computational rules—what you are doing is enabling the child to 'understand' what natural numbers are. . . . Somehow, the natural numbers are already 'there,' existing somewhere in the Platonic world and we have access to that world through our ability to be aware of things. If we were simply mindless computers, we would not have that ability."[10] Computers can do all sorts of fabulously complicated things but they don't *understand* anything. (Perhaps I should add that the highly publicized triumph of the computer, Big Blue, in a chess match with the world's champion, Gary Kasparov, does not constitute a demonstration of artificial intelligence. What it does show is that a team of gifted programmers working with an extremely powerful computer and an exact record of all of the moves the human champion had made in chess matches over the past five to ten years can instruct the machine how to foil the champion's intuitions of the possibilities inherent in a given situation on the chessboard, especially if the champion is denied any knowledge whatsoever of the moves the computer made in the games it played in preparing for the match. It wasn't the intelligence of the computer that defeated Kasparov, it was the eeriness of playing against an absolutely inscrutable, unknowable opponent who knew everything about him as a chess player.)

Penrose's quantum-based argument took up about two hundred pages in *Shadows of the Mind*. He achieves a shorter, easier-to-grasp statement of it in the third book, but I still wouldn't care to try to do more than give the nub of it: The fundamental processes of the brain take place at a subcellular level where classical, Newtonian physics makes no sense, where quantum physics prevails. That being true, the brain is nothing like a computer and any understanding of its workings lies beyond the reach of any computational scheme whatsoever. So much, if I may repeat myself, for the dreams of computational glory of the proponents of AI; but so much as well for all critical ideas that are based directly or indirectly on understandings of mind and behavior derived from computational, classical physics with its emphasis on simple cause-and-effect reasoning. If you think about it, that knocks the props out from under all the ideologically driven theories of criticism. Further, if Penrose

10. Roger Penrose, with Abner Shimony, Nancy Cartwright, and Stephen Hawking, *The Large, the Small, and the Human Mind*, 115–16.

is right, before we can hope to understand what is really going on in consciousness and intelligence, we will have to have a new physics that will give us a more profound understanding of matter, time, space, and the laws that govern them.

In all three of his books, Penrose calls for "a correct theory of quantum gravity" that will reconcile the apparent contradictions between the quantum theories that apply at the subcellular levels of the brain and the Newtonian theories that one must use in explaining the larger-scale operations of the nervous system. Penrose thinks, as do Stephen Hawking and other theoretical physicists, that its discovery is not far off and that it will incorporate the uncertainty principle. I doubt that anybody who hasn't done a good deal of work in quantum mechanics has any real grasp of that strange principle, but humanists could and should take it as a guiding metaphor and embrace as liberating the uncertainty of the arts they work with and of everything they think and say about them. That way lies reality.

3

Comforting Falsehoods, Inconvenient Truths

My modest and, I thought, obviously sensible venture in turning to the physical sciences for help in dealing with issues and problems currently pressing in on literary criticism produced bigger and sometimes more conclusive results than I had thought possible. The matter is so important that I want to recapitulate what I said in the last chapter, even at the risk of spreading boredom.

I initially went to the physicist Roger Penrose for help in dealing with what I thought were loose and extravagant discussions of the possibility of developing computers to the point they would possess not only intelligence, but consciousness. I can't claim that Penrose's refutation of the claims of proponents of "strong AI" is absolutely conclusive because some of them are still disputing it, but it persuades me and, I gather, a great many other observers. If he is right, as I think he is, that computers have to work algorithmically—that is, by following a set of instructions for making a computation—I know he is right that some aspects of human intelligence lie outside the domain of algorithms. Fine, that settles that issue to my satisfaction. But Penrose's argument goes beyond that to undermine all of the ideological, deterministic theories of behavior that have dominated critical thinking in the last few decades by showing that the brain's most fundamental processes are governed by the unruly laws of quantum physics, not by the tidy cause-and-effect laws of Newtonian physics. Work with Penrose and other modern physicists for a while and you *know* that old-fashioned "scientific" determinism is a dead duck; you also are fairly sure that literary criticism is going to have to follow the lead of quantum physics and embrace some kind of uncertainty principle. If you are bothered by what Leon Lederman, Nobel laureate and former director of Fermilab, terms the "spookiness" of quantum physics in his book *The God Particle*, take guidance from what happens on a pool table. Good players know that if they hit the cue ball so it strikes the object ball at the right speed and the right angle the object ball must go where they want it to go—pure Newtonian mechanics, pure determinism. They know that they can sometimes pull off a combination shot—that is, they can hit the cue ball into one object ball so it will strike another object ball and knock it into a pocket—especially if the two object balls are fairly close together and not too far from the pocket. On combination shots Newtonian analysis becomes hard to manage, and determinism, shaky. But the best players in the world cannot tell where the balls are going to go when they begin a game of nine-ball by driving the cue ball the length of the table into the "rack" of nine tightly packed balls. Here, Newtonian explanations are totally unmanageable, and determinism impossible. Figure it as you will, the truth is literary critics must learn to live with uncertainty as coolly as nine-ball players and physicists do.

Similarly, I went to Gerald M. Edelman's *Bright Air, Brilliant Fire* looking for some help in understanding how the brain really does work so that I could better judge the validity of some theories of language and came away with some very firm understandings of major problems confronting criticism. Edelman does demonstrate that the objectivist theories of language that have greatly influenced recent criticism are simply wrong; the mind does not and cannot possibly use language that way. However, he also goes a very long way towards finally settling old doubts about how something as immaterial as the mind could possibly arise from something as grossly material as the brain by tracing and explaining the evolutionary development of the brain. He also demonstrates that the processes of the brain are entirely organic and therefore nothing like the processes of computers (thereby settling any traces of doubt left over from Penrose's critique of AI). He gives further evidence that physical realities are problematic rather than determined and he establishes the idea that no two human beings are identical in their bodies, their minds, or their experience. And—in case all of that isn't enough—he demonstrates that a command of metaphor and narrative are essential for the operation of the mind.

I had the same sort of experience with J. Allan Hobson's *The Chemistry of Conscious States*. Looking to see if Hobson gave some support to Edelman's theory of how the brain functions, I found he not only did that, but he also clinched the argument that the brain and the mind are two aspects of the same thing. He also demolished the possibility of anything like a Freudian interpretation of dreams or of literature, demonstrated the fundamental role of storytelling in the mind's work, and put the finishing touches on the argument that the mind is such a marvelously unruly place no system of determinism will account for what happens there.

This is, of course, an oversimplified account of my venture in self-education. I did more reading than I have mentioned and some of it was harder going than I have suggested, but still I can truthfully say that I have never before gotten such large returns from such a modest investment of time and effort in books that were so readily available and so obviously pertinent to my fundamental concerns. You would think that my experience would be commonplace, that critic after critic would have looked towards the sciences for help in dealing with the very wide range of concerns that any energetic reading of literature inevitably generates. Not so. Not these days. Many of the most fashionable critics and presumably many of the most prestigious graduate schools have been busily cultivating extraordinary ignorance of basic scientific truths and even inculcating hostility to science itself.

Paul R. Gross and Norman Levitt (a marine biologist and a mathematician, respectively) have laid out the depressing evidence in *Higher Superstition: The Academic Left and Its Quarrels with Science*. They organize their discussion by doctrines: a chapter on cultural constructivism, another on postmodernism, then feminism, New Age millenarianism, and what they term "the schools of indictment," the gays and lesbians, the radical environmentalists, and the Afrocentrists, all of whom see science and technology as instruments of an unjust society. Gross and Levitt do not pick on academic small-fry; most of the people they name hold important positions in academia and most of the works they cite were published by university presses or in well-known journals. Nor do they pull their punches. To illustrate the arrant ignorance of prominent postmodernists they catch Jacques Derrida posturing about the mathematical field of topology and then confusing it with the geographical field of topography. They turn to a book, *Chaos Bound*, published by the Cornell University Press and written by a literary scholar, N. Katherine Hayles, whose specialty is the relations among science, literature, and contemporary literary theory. Hayles argues "for deep parallels and assonances between the mathematics of chaos and the theoretical practices of textual critics loyal to the tenets of postmodernism,"[1] but she displays, they demonstrate, a profound ignorance of mathematics and gross misunderstanding of ideas espoused by Bertrand Russell, Alfred North Whitehead, Albert Einstein, and Kurt Gödel. Even worse, I think, than such pretentious ignorance is the hostility of literary and social critics of various persuasions who attack "bourgeois-" or "masculine-" or "westernized-" or "capitalistic-" or some other evil brand of science and who are, apparently, too self-centered and smug to know that they are following hot in the footsteps of Hitler and Stalin, who condemned "Jewish science" and sought to murder its practitioners.

Gross and Levitt attribute the antiscientific attitudes and ideas they are analyzing to "the academic left." They have misgivings about that label, but writing before 1994 and wanting to keep their focus on the academic world, it made reasonable, if not perfect, sense. The attitudes did seem to have their roots in antiwar protests of the 1960s and the ideas in the writings of Nietzsche and Heidegger. But reading their book after 1994, after the appearance on the political scene of Newt Gingrich and his band of supporters in the House of Representatives who describe themselves as *"radical* Republicans," that label and that analysis just won't do. Nobody has ever accused them or their "Christian conservative" allies of being on the left, let alone of reading Nietzsche and Heidegger, yet they promote know-nothing attitudes towards science just as vigorously as the academics do, often in similar or the same terms. Gross and Levitt's statement of what defines the academic left is one that the radical Republicans would be glad to claim for themselves: "a deep concern with cultural issues, and, in particular, a commitment to the idea that fundamental political change is urgently needed and can be achieved only through revolutionary processes rooted in a wholesale revision of cultural categories."[2] Whatever it is at

1. Paul R. Gross and Norman Levitt, *Higher Superstition: The Academic Left and Its Quarrels with Science*, 98–99.
2. Ibid., 3.

the roots of the postmodernist-feminist-environmentalist-New Age scorn of scientific ideas and attitudes and achievements that Gross and Levitt describe is something that's all over the place, not just on the left or the right of some mythical political center. I would like to call it ideology, but I had better explain the sense in which I am using the term, for it can be confusing.

The *American Heritage Dictionary* offers two quite different definitions for it: "1. The body of ideas reflecting the social needs and aspirations of an individual, a group, a class, or a culture. 2. A set of doctrines or beliefs forming the basis of a political or economic system." That order suggests that the first idea is the dominant one in current usage. The *Oxford Concise Dictionary* gives essentially the same definitions but reverses the order. Other desk dictionaries give those definitions sometimes in the one order, sometimes the other. The *OED* manages to fuse the two senses but stresses that an ideology is "a systematic scheme of ideas . . . especially one that is held implicitly or adopted as a whole and maintained regardless of the course of events." Personally, I am glad to accept the *OED*'s stress, but I observe that some careful writers do not. I noted that in the several dictionaries I looked at the example always given for ideology as a set of doctrines was "Marxist ideology"; for ideology as a loose body of ideas the example always was "bourgeois ideology." I don't really know which meaning developed first but those examples suggest that the "strict" sense came first and was applied pejoratively; the second sense, I would like to think, came later and was generated by adherents to a strict set of doctrines as a defensive gambit. The Marxists have been particularly fond of muddying words that way, but practically every other ideologist who wants to avoid a stigma uses the same device. It's like a game of Ping-Pong: you comment to a feminist about the narrowness of certain feminist views, and you'll promptly hear of the notorious narrowness of the critics of feminism. I take a slightly dizzy way out of all of this confusion. Everyone agrees with the definition that the *American Heritage* gives for "ideologue": "An advocate of a particular ideology, especially an official exponent of that ideology." And it is generally taken as a pejorative term; I have never heard of anyone boasting about being an ideologue, except, of course, for functionaries of totalitarian governments, who seem more like zombies than human beings.

Let it be understood, then, that when I refer to ideologies I am referring to the sorts of ideas promulgated by ideologues. Deconstructionism, I think, is an ideology, and Fascism certainly was one; since Paul De Man celebrated Fascism early in his life and deconstructionism late, I think it fair to term him an ideologue. Walker Percy was so full of ideas that he made novels out of them, but his theory of language is untainted by ideology. His friend Shelby Foote is an even more spectacular example of the writer who is free of ideology. His superbly balanced narrative history of the Civil War fills three long volumes, each one a model of understanding grounded in facts and illuminated by imagination. Foote is so free of ideological bias that he came to the conclusion that the two most gifted men involved in the war were Abraham Lincoln and Nathan Bedford Forrest, the author of the Emancipation Proclamation and a former slave-dealer.

It seems to me that in recent years we have been peculiarly, oppressively beset by ideologies and their true believers. That's probably not true; I am probably guilty, as most of us are inclined to be, of exaggerating and romanticizing the difficulties of my own times. No doubt pernicious doctrines and their servants have flourished in most times and in lots of places. Still, we do have a nasty problem on hand: public discourse on the arts or on any other subject worth thinking about has the function of clarifying misunderstandings and reaching conclusions that can be regarded as truthful—or at least as truthful for the time being, until circumstances change and we come to know more about the matter—but in our time we are bombarded with public discourse that avoids clarifications and prefers make-believe to truth. The out-and-out propaganda, the campaign speeches of those who would claim leadership of this group or that, we can deal with fairly easily; our trouble comes from intellectuals and professors we think we can trust who would rather peddle comforting falsehoods than confront inconvenient truths. Some of those peddlers can be quite illustrious.

For highly illustrious, still often-admired examples, take Jean-Paul Sartre and Simone de Beauvoir. As Tony Judt has explained in well-documented detail in *Past Imperfect: French Intellectuals, 1944–1956*, they managed to convince themselves that the murderous horrors of Stalinist rule in the Soviet Union and in Central and Eastern Europe in the years immediately following the end of the war in

Europe were neither murderous nor horrible and did their eloquent best to persuade others to share that astonishing conviction. They had a good deal of company among leftist French intellectuals, especially other contributors to *Les Temps Modernes* and contributors to Emmanuel Mounier's Catholic journal, *Ésprit;* but most of the others fell by the wayside in the fifties while Sartre and de Beauvoir kept the faith even after 1956 (when Khrushchev officially denounced Stalin's crimes and the Soviet army brutally crushed uprisings in Poland and Hungary) and well into the sixties. In the early fifties, Sartre announced, "I have looked, but I just cannot find any evidence of an aggressive impulse on the part of the Russians in the last three decades," and in 1963, he amazed an audience of Czech students and intellectuals in Prague by singing the praises of literature that conformed to the ideals of socialist realism. It wasn't until December 1968, months after the Soviet tanks rolled into Prague, that he finally broke with the Communists. Mme de Beauvoir contributed numerous politically correct essays to *Les Temps Modernes,* managing, for example, to defend capital punishment in the Soviet Union, to describe *Shane* and *High Noon* as military propaganda designed to prepare Western audiences for a "preventive war," and to dismiss the writings of intellectuals like Viktor Kravchenko and Arthur Koestler who had survived firsthand experience of Communist camps and prisons as mere storytelling.[3] She, too, stayed on until 1968. All in all, the two of them achieved an impressive record for mendacity.

Had Sartre and de Beauvoir been ordinary party hacks there would be nothing surprising about their prolonged refusal to find any fault with the Soviet Union, but they claimed to be clear and independent thinkers, not party hacks, and were among the most celebrated proponents of existentialism. Sartre presented himself as a philosopher of that movement and they both gloried in their fame as intellectuals articulating the need for the ever-solitary individual to take responsibility for the authenticity of his or her own actions. Judt is properly contemptuous of their utter failure to test their political thought against political reality as their philosophy said they should. When it came to politics, never mind authenticity, they voted for the comforts of make-believe, though the stench

3. Tony Judt, *Past Imperfect: French Intellectuals, 1944–1956,* 154, 92, 178, 155.

surrounding that particular bit of make-believe was powerful. Intellectuals are like fishmongers; they are supposed to make certain that none of the goods they sell have gone rotten. The Stalinism Sartre and de Beauvoir peddled was one rotten fish.

You never really know why anybody does anything, but plausible explanations of why they, and many other French intellectuals of their time, made this terrible blunder are available; they come in layers. First and most obviously, Sartre, de Beauvoir, and the others had always disliked the English and they despised the Americans for having offended French pride by so noisily doing for them what they hadn't been able to do for themselves, liberate France from the Germans. One can't begrudge them some resentment; when Americans get to swaggering, as we did in 1944–1945, we get hard to take, offending (as the French would have it) the *amour propre* of everybody around us. For French intellectuals to exaggerate the role they themselves played in the liberation was only human, but when they went on first to minimize the American role in it and then, after the war, to put all of the blame for the Cold War on America and none on Russia, they crossed the border into paranoia and falsehood.

French history made it easier to go that way. In the 1930s French politics were a mess. The government of the Third Republic was at best weak and inept, and at fairly frequent worst, corrupt. Right-wing intellectuals like Charles Maurras, the founder and guiding spirit of the *Action française* movement, exerted a large and poisonous influence on domestic political affairs, and fascism was flourishing all over Europe. In such circumstances it is no wonder that so many of the best of the young intellectuals just coming on the scene pinned their hopes on policies and parties sympathetic to communism. That the French educational system had ground into them a strong preference for either-or structures of thought made it easier to pin their hopes in the first place and harder to unpin them when circumstances later changed.

Still, the argument of "the times" won't do to excuse, let alone explain, why such extraordinarily brilliant people as Sartre, de Beauvoir, and their friends so willfully persisted in preferring simple falsehoods to complicated truths. On the particular matter of rationalizing away any objections to judicial murder in the show trials in Moscow and Prague or to the bloody repressions on the streets of

Warsaw and Budapest, the history of the French Revolution with its sanction of terror gives us a way of understanding, though not of excusing. French intellectuals grew up memorizing Robespierre and Saint-Just on how the rights of individuals must yield to the rights of the people rather than Thomas Jefferson on how governments are instituted among men to secure the individual's rights to life, liberty, and the pursuit of happiness. The French have never had anything like a Jeffersonian vision of the paramount importance of the individual; they have never had any experience, Judt says, with liberal democracy and the sorts of laws and social attitudes that go with it. Nonetheless, in the fifties, most Frenchmen, including intellectuals like Albert Camus, François Mauriac, and Raymond Aron, did not follow Sartre and the others down the path of blind loyalty to a totalitarianism that claimed to act in the name of the people, perhaps because they were busy participating in the socioeconomic transformation that was sweeping over France; the French Communist Party and its existentialist admirers apparently didn't notice that was happening.

Judt means that quite literally; Sartre and the others apparently didn't see what was going on all around them as postwar prosperity and postwar technology blossomed in France. The new cars, clothes, houses, highways, shops, and factories didn't attract much of their attention; the effects of better diets and better medical care visible on the faces of children and their parents didn't register on them. The changes that increasing economic security and relative prosperity wrought on the social and political attitudes of masses of people didn't mean enough to them to affect their thinking. They preferred to elaborate the ramifications of a philosophy that conceived of human existence in a peculiarly abstract way. Sartre's disdain for America's role in the liberation of France could not have stood up to the experience of walking through the American cemetery overlooking Omaha Beach nor could his celebration of Soviet peacefulness have withstood the experience of fingering the scars left on the buildings and streets of Budapest by Soviet tanks in 1956. But Sartre didn't look at crosses by the thousand in cemeteries any more than he touched the handiwork of tanks; he didn't deal in perceptions of concrete things, only in the manipulation of abstractions.

All intellectuals are liable to fall into the habit of excessively abstract thinking, but French intellectuals do seem to be more liable than most. (I will consider a few of our homegrown abstractionists later in this chapter.) Judt suggests that the long effort of the guardians of the French language to preserve it from pollution by other languages or by the French of uneducated speakers has worked to permit or even to encourage French intellectuals to cultivate abstract styles of thought and argument unchecked by any concern for vulgar, concrete reality. It is much harder to remain so abstractly refined in English, which is wide open to every breeze that blows, from either abroad or below. Judt suggests further that the tendency towards unqualified abstractness has been reinforced by the custom in Sartre's time and even after the war for graduates of the *École normale supérieure,* the training ground of French intellectuals, to spend some postgraduate time studying German philosophy in Berlin. Sartre and, much later, Jacques Derrida came away pumped full of Hegel, Nietzche, and Heidegger, so full they had trouble digesting it all. One suspects that their German wasn't quite up to the task of mastering such highly, not to say wildly, Germanic material. (The spectacle of monolingual Americans getting their German philosophy by way of English translations of Derrida's French is pure farce.)

Finally, after considering all of the probable explanations why Sartre or any other intellectual comes down so squarely, so blatantly on the side of falsehood, one has to ask, what was the *quid pro quo* here? What did the intellectual derive from the bargain? Or, in good vulgar American, what was in it for him? The answer must be speculative, of course, but one must note that their prolonged loyalty to communism guaranteed Sartre and de Beauvoir that an audience and some number of admiring critics would come from the ranks of fellow loyalists; perhaps more importantly, their anti-Americanism gave them a reliable source of prestige and distinction among the very many chauvinists in French intellectual life who feared the encroachment of American ways on French culture. (The French Academy sought to prohibit use of such borrowings from American as *le weekend,* and proper commentators regularly bewailed the appearance of hamburgers and Coca-Cola in French diets. Nobody had to fear the impact of Russian on the language or of caviar on the diet.) To borrow a line from Vladimir Nabokov, you could count on the fingers of one maimed hand the number of intellectuals who are not concerned about their audience and their prestige.

It is hard to have much respect for anybody who so plainly—so knowingly—supports falsehoods; I find it impossible to respect people like Sartre and de Beauvoir who have trained intellects and a public obligation to think clearly when the falsehood they are purveying has meant murderous oppression to others while they live cosseted lives. Perhaps my low opinion of them as persons should be held quite separate from my judgment of their work as writers. Perhaps. But if the work of fools is foolishness, the work of ideologues is ideology, and I dislike ideology at least as much as I dislike foolishness. I think Tony Judt takes a similar position; certainly he has a low opinion of the thought and writing of both Sartre and de Beauvoir. Josef Skvorecky might have an even lower opinion of Sartre, for he had to endure the oppression in Prague while Sartre was safe in Paris endorsing it. His account in *The Miracle Game* of the fatuous performance at an international literary conference in Vienna in the mid-sixties of a critic who spouts the literary theories of Robbe-Grillet, and therefore could fit nicely into Sartre's circle of admirers, is a model of well-tempered satire. But Milan Kundera, who also had the educational experience of living in communist Czechoslovakia while first reading Sartre, manages in *Testaments Betrayed* to firmly separate the socialist propagandist from the existentialist philosopher and novelist. Of course, when Kundera went into exile he settled in Paris, where he has moved in the highest intellectual circles, and Skvorecky settled in Toronto, where he taught American literature at a branch of the University of Toronto.

Some of the reviews of *Past Imperfect* are worth noting for what they show of the attitudes of contemporary English-speaking intellectuals towards Sartre's cultivation of falsehood. John Sturrock, reviewing in the *New York Times Book Review*, came down squarely on the side of falsehood. He didn't think it quite fair to judge Sartre harshly just because he excused the Czech Party bosses for the show trial that led to the hanging of Rudolph Slansky and thirteen other government officials, all of whom were Jews, on the grounds that "justice" is what those in power think it ought to be. Indeed, Sturrock describes Judt as "a sharp, even a vindictive moralist" because he would indict intellectuals for "failing to test their political thought against political reality"; he himself admits to a feeling of nostalgia for the good old days when he was a student in France and public life there was enlivened by "talented and rampaging ideologues like Sartre."[4]

Paul Berman, reviewing in the *New Yorker*, was not quite so startlingly amoral. He danced around the implications of the book Judt wrote to gesture at the much more urbane book he would have written himself. Berman's hypothetical book would have preserved respect for the "genius" and "spirit" of the French writers while of course reproving them for their occasional excesses in serving the cause of anti-anticommunism.[5]

John Weightman, in the *New York Review of Books*, stood in sharp contrast to Sturrock and Berman, summarizing Judt's book clearly and accurately, and giving carefully reasoned arguments for valuing it highly. Yet at one point Weightman flirts with disaster by asserting that it is "a very peculiar circumstance" that somebody possessed of a brain as impressive as Sartre's could be "so monstrously biased."[6] No, it is not; not at all. The truth is that despite the power of their brains, intellectuals are no better and no worse than anybody else, only a lot more articulate. They are simply very good at spinning out reasons for doing whatever they want to do, even— or perhaps especially—when they want to do something monstrous. They deserve to be called "mouthpieces" every bit as much as lawyers do, for in the last few hundred years they have proved to be, I am very sorry to say, every bit as likely as lawyers to indulge in dishonest, self-serving, client-flattering pleadings.

For a purely American—and quite farcical—demonstration of intellectuals in love with falsehood consider the highly publicized affair of the hoax that the physicist Alan Sokal palmed off on the editors of *Social Text*, a journal of "cultural studies," for their Spring/Summer 1996 issue and revealed in the May/June issue of *Lingua Franca* that was published the same day. The hoax took the form of a burlesque article entitled "Transgressing the Boundaries: Toward a Transformative Hermeneutics of Quantum Gravity" that drew various cultural, philosophical, and political morals that Sokal judged would appeal to the prejudices of people who were fashionably fond of questioning the claims of science to objectivity. He

4. John Sturrock, "The Last Days of the Intellocrats."
5. Paul Berman, "Paris Follies."
6. John Weightman, "Fatal Attraction."

played fair with the editors; though he cultivated the tone of their typical articles with deadpan accuracy, he larded the piece with howlers of various sorts that would have been caught by anybody who read it at all carefully. I mean, a bland reference to pi as a variable ought to raise suspicions in a moderately bright high school student and a series of preposterous statements about "linear" mathematics, relativity, and quantum mechanics ought to raise the hair on the head of anybody who knows enough about modern science to discuss its role in contemporary culture. Apparently, the editors were so excited by the thought that they had found a real, live *physicist* who would publish with them that they weren't about to fuss over the details of his article. Once the issue came off the press, Sokal was free to reveal the hoax in *Lingua Franca,* comfortably certain that he had exposed the editors' willingness to swallow any kind of nonsense that flattered their ideological preconceptions.

But that was merely the beginning; the truly farcical developments followed. First, the editors issued a statement defending their decision to publish the piece and one of them even had the *chutzpah* to suggest that the supposed parody had not been intended as a parody and that Sokal's denunciation of it in *Lingua Franca* actually represented a loss of intellectual determination. Then, Stanley Fish, the executive director of the Duke University Press, which publishes *Social Text,* Professor of Law and of English at Duke University, and boss promoter of American postmodernism, denounced Sokal's "bad joke" at great length in an op-ed article in the *New York Times* employing his standard technique for dealing with criticism: first, a flat denial of the charge that sociologists and humanists who speak of science as a "social construction" see science as merely a social construction, then a shift of emphasis to wonder why Sokal is attacking the innocent, and finally an extended exercise in spurious either-or logic, in this case an argument that baseball and science are both social constructions, both fit subjects for sociological study.[7] (This is the same man who reportedly wrote a letter to the dean of his college requesting that a member of the English Department who had joined the National Association of Scholars be barred from serving on tenure and hiring committees, and subsequently at a meeting of his peers in the department

7. Stanley Fish, "Professor Sokal's Bad Joke."

denied ever having written the letter, even though each person at the meeting was holding a xeroxed copy of it.)

Sokal thought he was merely exposing the intellectual defects of the people responsible for *Social Text*; it turns out he was giving them a chance to renew their pledge of allegiance to falsehood. Exhibitionists that they are, they were not about to pass up the opportunity. Stanley Fish did not attain his position of prominence in the academic world by cultivating shyness; he is a showman of the most brazen sort. He and his colleagues at *Social Text* are good for a derisive laugh as they promote themselves to positions of notoriety in the shrinking company of those who still take postmodernism seriously, but Sartre and his friends constitute a more resistant and finally much more revealing subject of study.

To return, Judt's "essay on intellectual irresponsibility" (as he calls it) does a handsomely solid job of giving a general reader an understanding of the hows and whys of the folly of the French intellectuals in the postwar period. Judt places it so carefully in the web of their lives, works, and culture that you can't escape developing some understanding of it, even while shaking your head in dismay, and that understanding in turn pushes you some way down the track towards understanding the way other bright people in other times and places dealing with other issues persist in believing the unbelievable, in treasuring what ought to be true rather than what is true. Personally, I find it fairly easy to understand why they do it; vanity, greed, ambition, and the various brands of lust will account for behavior a lot stranger than that. But how they do it is a more puzzling matter. How do people with strong, well-trained minds manage to persuade themselves to go against all their training and embrace false conclusions? And even more, how do they manage to do it in perfect silence, without letting, so to speak, the left brain know what the right brain is doing?

The most reliable method, I suppose, is the time-tested one of true believers: they defer in fundamental matters to some higher power, whether a church or a party, a prophet or a führer, doesn't matter as long as they are given someone to identify with and a few dogmas to rely on or a party line to follow. The beauty of such an arrangement for intellectuals is that it relieves them of complex responsibilities while freeing them to make profitable use of their minds in other, lesser matters. Some contemporary academics have created a special variation on this classic arrangement by making, in effect, a religion out of science and then by insisting that the only truly scientific conclusions are those that can be stated objectively in mathematical terms. That permitted behavioral psychologists to deny the reality of consciousness and social psychologists to think that their opinion polls have validity because the results they generate can be expressed statistically.

True believing, though, involves a consciousness of the faith as something that can be chosen; it is a little too aware of what it is up to, a little too liable to hypocritical exploitation. To account for the blind, persistent preference for make-believe that renders so much contemporary discourse futile, we need to locate a cause that can be described as perfectly unconscious or at least perfectly ignorant. I think that John Searle has done just that in *The Rediscovery of the Mind* by focusing on the currently commonplace objection of intellectuals that language is inherently so indeterminate in its meanings as to be incapable of expressing thought accurately. That is the notion that licenses critics to "deconstruct" the writing of others (they get nasty if anybody tries to deconstruct what they themselves have written). It is a fairly silly notion, as Searle demonstrates, grounded in ignorance of how all languages work and in fantastical vanity about the intellectual capacities of critics. Of course words are indeterminate, but that doesn't mean that the language is unworthy of the critics who must use it. Words can and frequently do carry two or more meanings at once because they have to, for people have to communicate with each other about a reality that generally carries several implications at once.

That point is enough to skewer the deconstructionists, but Searle carries the matter one crucially important step further: he recognizes that sentences, not words, are the basic unit of meaning in ordinary discourse and coolly insists that "sentence meaning *radically* underdetermines the content of what is said."[8] Take a very simple set of words, using them as literally as possible; put them into the simplest kind of syntactical structure; and you will have a statement that depends for its full meaning on matters not even hinted at in the sentence. To use Searle's example, in the sentence "I have had breakfast," no mention is made of time, but people would normally and

8. John Searle, *The Rediscovery of the Mind*, 181 (his emphasis).

correctly understand it to mean that the speaker has had breakfast today, very likely some time this morning. Searle's term for the range of human capacities (abilities, know-hows, customs, etc.) that complete the meaning of sentences is *Background*, with a capital *B* to indicate that he is using the word in a somewhat technical way. It's an interesting concept that Searle developed earlier and exploits in *The Rediscovery of the Mind*. For me it's a useful explanation of both how language communicates meaning by leaving much of it unstated and why it needs to do so if it is to communicate at all (because if you felt that you had to specify all of the possibly necessary qualifications to a statement you wouldn't have the time and energy to complete it). More importantly for my purposes here, if you turn the emphasis the other way, you can see, very clearly, how otherwise intelligent people can manage to believe not merely false but downright crazy propositions simply by ignoring or distorting the appropriate Background of a statement. Somebody could take the epigraph of *Walden*, "I do not propose to write an ode to dejection, but to brag as lustily as Chanticleer in the morning, standing on his roost, if only to wake my neighbors up," as evidence of Thoreau's egregious male egotism—if he or she could manage to avoid knowing that the loudest, ugliest, silliest, and most irritating sound emanating from the backyards of nineteenth-century villages was the crow of a rooster and at the same time avoid knowing that with his big nose and short stature Thoreau could be said to look like a rooster. Or, to go back to Judt's intellectuals, they could applaud the Communist-sponsored Peace Congress in Paris in April 1949, because they could treat the Soviet Union's brutal takeover of Czechoslovakia in February 1948 as a benign extension of protection to a people whose peace was threatened by American aggression.

Searle's emphasis on the role of Background in completing the meaning of statements turns out to be, finally, an insistence on the necessity of placing statements, no matter how purely abstract or analytical they may seem to be, in the context of an unspoken narrative element. (As a character in James Gould Cozzens's novel *Guard of Honor* observes, "Few ideas could be abstract enough to be unqualified by the company they kept.")[9] The statement "I have had breakfast" means what it means because the speaker can assume

9. James Gould Cozzens, *Guard of Honor*, 68.

that the listener also knows the "story" of breakfast, the first meal of the day, usually a simple one needing no talking about. Contrastingly, the full meaning of the statement "I am having root-canal work done on my molar" (as in fact I was at the time of writing this) will remain in considerable doubt until I make clear my sense of the "story" of dental work. Since that is a threatening story for many people, I should hasten to add that I found the experience more tedious than painful, dentists and dental equipment having improved tremendously since the bad old days. Effectiveness as either a writer or a reader, a speaker or a listener, requires skill and judgment in dealing with Background and its narrative implications. Writers and speakers who have a poor sense of the stories behind their statements seem dull, clumsy, and unclear; readers and listeners who are not responsive to stories botch their understanding of whatever they are reading or hearing.

The similarity of the distinction that Searle makes between "deep" and "local" Background to the distinction rhetoricians have long made between denotative and connotative meanings goes directly to the center of the main issue of my opening chapters.[10] It suggests, quite rightly, that something like Background is operative at the level of words as well as at the level of statements or, to put it less technically, that words as well as statements evoke narrative elements that are essential to their full meaning. Dictionary entries can capture the denotative meaning of words, but any attempt to get at connotative meaning must at least adumbrate a story because connotative meanings are the products of the experiences people have had with the things the words refer to. Those experiences may often have been messy and emotional and therefore distasteful to pedantic rationalists, but they are real and they have to be dealt with. Anyone who ignores them, who finds it beneath his analytical dignity to cultivate a sensitivity to narrative, is dooming himself to foolishness. The ability to tell and to read stories (using that term in its broadest, least professionalized sense) is as much a function of intelligence as the ability to work with abstract ideas.

Jean-Paul Sartre and Simone de Beauvoir were commonly acclaimed for their brilliance, but they were not storytellers, even though a number of their books have to be classified as novels.

10. Searle, *Rediscovery*, 194.

Albert Camus may not have graduated from the *École normale supérieure*, but he was a storyteller who wrote novels that will not go away. (He was also Tony Judt's source for the epigraph for *Past Imperfect*: "Mistaken ideas always end in bloodshed, but in every case it is someone else's blood. That is why some of our thinkers feel free to say just about anything.") The ability to tell and to respond to stories is an essential quality of a strong mind; nonetheless, the woods are full of intellectuals who ignore or deny the power of and necessity for stories. Ignorant of stories themselves, they would breed the same ignorance in generations of students. People who deny the power of stories are cultivating stupidity in one important part of their minds, and stupidity is indeed what flourishes there, no matter how dazzling their scores on IQ tests may be. Stupidity, as a matter of course and with remarkable consistency, generates a preference for comforting falsehoods over inconvenient truths.

4

"Tell Me a Story, Daddy"

John Searle's idea about Background may not look like much sitting on the page. Its primary parts are simple and even obvious, once Searle has stated them. Sentences, not words, are the basic unit of meaning—most of us know that in our bones, though we may weakly submit when linguists, whose concern is with language, not with communication, carry on about words and signs as primary carriers of meaning. Searle's assertion that sentences radically underdetermine meaning seems a bit surprising until he completes his idea by observing that the implied Background of a sentence plays a major role in determining its meaning. By *Background* he means, as I have noted, the capacities, abilities, and knowledge that are necessary to formulating the actions and intentions the sentence deals with. In other and still simpler terms, Searle is saying a sentence asserts only part of what it means; the rest of it has to be understood. We all do understand and act on that notion; if we didn't, we couldn't talk to each other. Do not misunderstand me as belittling Searle's accomplishment in working out his theory; it is the nature of creative insights, as Arthur Koestler explained in *The Act of Creation*, to be obvious once they have finally been made. ("Of course, Herr Gutenberg, printers need presses like the wine makers use." "Naturally, Mr. Newton, something is pulling things to fall always down, never up.") The real power of the idea doesn't become clear until you take it off the page, so to speak, and apply it to a set of actual circumstances, as I did in the last chapter when it answered easily and clearly the otherwise baffling question of how brilliant people manage to believe stupid and ghastly falsehoods, Jean-Paul Sartre and Simone de Beauvoir being two conveniently obvious examples with their long-held belief in a benign Soviet

Union. Using it as a critical tool in dealing with works of literature gets some equally powerful results.

I want to take for test purposes the second and third chapters of George V. Higgins's novel, *Sandra Nichols Found Dead*, which are so vivid and strong that they could almost stand alone; I can concentrate on them without having to get into much summary of the novel as a whole. The subject of these two chapters is Detective Lieutenant Royce Whitlock of the Massachusetts State Police, one of the major characters in the novel; the narrator-hero, Jerry Kennedy, is striving to get a sense of his character and abilities because Jerry is under heavy pressure to accept appointment to represent in probate court three children, whose mother's death Whitlock has been investigating ever since her body was found in a swamp stuffed in a plastic trash bag five months after she disappeared. Whitlock is convinced that her wealthy husband had her murdered, though he can't get enough evidence to prove it in a criminal court; the judge in charge of the case in probate court puts the finger on Jerry as a lawyer who might be able to win in civil court an action for wrongful death and at least secure the children's financial future. Jerry, who would much rather be doing something else, has to decide if Whitlock can and will get him enough evidence to win what is bound to be a difficult action. The first of the two chapters deals with what Jerry learns about Whitlock; the second with what he learns from Whitlock. Both chapters, the second one especially, make flamboyant use of the skill in rendering American speech that Higgins has been developing and refining in the twenty-five years since he published his first novel, *The Friends of Eddie Coyle*. I shall quote from them extensively, as much, possibly, for the pleasure of doing so as for the necessity.

Whitlock, who is fifty-one and about to become eligible for retirement from the state police, is an extreme case; a dogged, methodical investigator who hates loose ends so much that he spends nearly all of his time making sure he hasn't overlooked anything in any of his investigations. He indulges in only two passions, photography and saving money, so that when he retires he'll be able to indulge a third passion, travel to all of the places he has always wanted to visit. He seems to be a classic obsessive personality, not merely thrifty but fabulously, proudly cheap; yet unlike most obsessive types he also possesses a harsh, self-judging sense of humor. Southeast Asia is the one part of the world he will not travel to in retirement, he explains, because he was there with the navy SEALs, underwater demolitions experts.

I've seen enough of that to last me a good long time, buncha little yellow guys in black pajamas, wearin' sandals they made outta tire carcasses, poppin' up all the time out of tunnels they dug in the ground right under my feet and trying to blow my ass off. Just because I was in their country, tryin' to send them to Buddha. People say they've forgiven us now, but I dunno, I'm not sure. I'm not goin' back to that place. Goin' other places, such as Ireland, where I've never even been, so nobody hates me there yet, and I can take pictures of them. Hard to take good pictures, concentrate and all on your composition and the lighting, so forth, when someone's tryin', shoot you.[1]

His second wife, Agnes, is his match in every way except cheapness. She puts up, she explains to Jerry, with his cheapness because he was a perfect stepfather and male model for her two boys

after their rat-bastard father disappeared and never even saw them, got in touch with them again. Can you beat that? Just *took off*, God only knows where he went to. And then they never heard from him again. Can you *imagine* a man doing that? What kind of a man would do that? Leave his wife, maybe, sure, I can understand that; maybe I did drive him nuts. But just to walk away from his own kids like that? What kind of a father does that? It isn't a natural thing. But he did it, the bastard, and I got to admit I dunno what would've happened to those two kids of mine, they'd've been left with just me. . . . [Royce] never had kids of his own. But he never let that stop him, get in his way—nope, he was a champion dad. My God, but he was a prince. So I'll forgive him a lot for that, for what he did for the boys. He can be tighter'n a Pullman window, but he *never* was cheap with the boys.[2]

Still she has misgivings about his obsessive stinginess, which seems to be getting worse as he gets older. She says that he

might be going to have a lot of trouble getting over being cheap—which is really his *main* hobby, you know, being tighter'n the childproof caps on aspirin bottles—when the day comes to cash in and take all those trips he's always saying're the reason for it, and then the question's gonna have to be: "Well, all well and good, but will he be able to do it?" And if he doesn't do it, like he's said so long we're going to; if after we've been through all of this, then we *don't* get to Glacier National Park and the Painted Desert; the Atlas Mountains in

1. George V. Higgins, *Sandra Nichols Found Dead*, 6.
2. Ibid., 6–7.

Morocco; Iceland; the west of Ireland; take those trips and all; if it's all been just talk to camouflage the miser's work, or he's dead from a stroke, or all crippled up, so he can't go no place anymore, any way, so the money just stays in the bank, well, I ask you: What am I going to do then? I won't have no choice, will I, now? If that's it then I'm going to have to kill him. Just take his damned gun and shoot him. It's just as simple as that. And I don't mind telling you: I worry about it; I worry about it a *lot*.[3]

All that and more is in the second chapter. The third chapter consists solely of Whitlock's monologue—or better, I think, aria—on the murder of Sandra Nichols that he's sure, though he can't quite prove it, her third husband, Peter Wade, was responsible for. He is explaining to Jerry Kennedy why he is dragging him into the case. He starts out complaining that Peter Wade is

not a good man, not by any means. He's lazy and he's oversexed. His family spoiled him, growing up, and he's pampered himself ever since. . . . He's like one of those people you don't see so many of around much anymore, you know? Useless people. Ornaments, but Christmas's long ago over, tree's been taken down and gone to the dump. This time it's not coming back. So they stay useless, the rest of their lives, unless they get worse, and restless, so they do some actual damage. Which appears to be what he did. They don't really go out of their way to actually *bother* anyone, but they bother them just the same. Just by the way they carry themselves, their whole attitude thing, you know? They don't do *anything* but just the same they're annoying. One of them comes around where you can see him, he really gets on your nerves. Like one of those big fat houseflies, kind with those shiny green wings? Makes a lot of softish noise, gets on your nerves, just having the bastard just buzzing around. Really pisses you off.[4]

Then, like a tenor in the opera, he goes to the front of the stage to elaborate on the theme of the uselessness of such people.

Peter Wade's like that, once something's happened and he's gotten into your life. After that you're gonna sort of always be *aware* of him, always aware he's around. Like one of those ugly Civil War monuments, or a stone wall. Only his kind're more like the fly: he doesn't stay put. His kind doesn't stay in one place. They pop up, time to time, in various places, and even though they're always the same, for some reason you're always surprised. Not that you *should* be

3. Ibid., 9–10.
4. Ibid., 16–23; the next several quotations are from these pages.

surprised; you should've known that they would. Like Joie Chitwood and His Hell-Drivers. You go to a fairgrounds in August, you should expect to find them there, putting on a big show. Because that's what it is that they do. Or used to do anyway—I don't know if they're still at it now. But *why* they do it—except for the money, which certainly is a good reason, or at least a good reason for them—why sane people pay them their *money* to do it: that is quite a different matter.

Then they are like swimmers:

People who swam the English Channel. See who could do it the fastest. . . . You'd see them in the Movietone News, when I was a little kid. . . . There'd be this funny-looking woman, or a man with a little jockstrap kind of thing on, a bathing cap, always looking very awkward. And also like they're freezing their asses off, in black-and-white, on Dover Beach or someplace. . . . There was a woman named Gertrude Something-or-Other—Ederle? Looked like somebody's mother: she did it a lot. And then there was another one did it absolutely naked, and there she was, a picture of her, getting ready to do it, right in front of you, and you *knew*, the guy'd just *told* you, she didn't have a suit on. Oh-boy, oh-boy . . . oh, *boy*, because you couldn't see a thing. Not even a nipple protrusion. She was all covered over with this black axle grease or something, black thick grease to keep her warm while she swam bare-ass to France. Bogus albino walrus with black fat on the outside: that was what she was. Eleanor Holm, I think her name was. Came back here and got married to some guy or other, run one of those fuckin' big-time nightclubs in New York. Former big speakeasy guy—now what the hell was *his* name? Now I'll be up all night, trying to remember that. And I remember thinking even then, even when I was a little kid, even if I couldn't see her nipples: "What the hell is this *for? What the hell *good* is this? Why are they all doing this thing? Who *cares* who can swim the fastest? Just what the hell is this shit *for* that they are all doing here?"

Then the theme shifts to Peter Wade's essentially disorderly ways, not that he's ever been arrested for being disorderly, but if he ever were he'd be sure to be able to bribe his way out of it. "What I'm saying is that there isn't any kind of *shape* to his life, you know? There isn't any order in it, and it doesn't seem to bother him, way it'd bother you or me. He's not *about* anything." And so on about the way Peter Wade goes careening around the world, completely out of control, constantly picking up things that might come in handy later.

Like his lawyer, Arthur Dean. The man is an absolute *shit* and Peter knows this. But shit or not, he looked like he might come in handy some day, and now that day's here, and he has. . . . I don't like people like that. I don't like people like Peter Wade is. I got a prejudice against them. Wait 'til the Mass. Commission Against Discrimination find out about that one, huh? I'll be up on charges, you bet. STATE POLICE DETECTIVE ADMITS PREJUDICE AGAINST KILLERS. KILLER ACTIVISTS OUTRAGED.

He is positive that Wade paid somebody to bash his wife's head in with a blunt object, stuff her in a garbage bag, and throw her away in a swamp just in order to avoid a very expensive divorce; the trouble is he knows that he can't prove it. He imagines what would be said if he urged the district attorney of Essex or of Exeter County to go get an indictment anyway, just on the chance that the added pressure would cause Wade to break: "I'm hearing this? With my shell-pink ears? From Royce *Whitlock*, I'm hearing *this*? I should get a murder-one indictment? In a case I know going in I can't prove?" Followed by mock-earnest advice on his need to get a really good rest for himself. He knows he can't do it, but the more he knows about Sandra Nichols's hard life the more he respects her, especially for all that she did through three bad marriages to make a decent life for her three kids. That, finally, is why he is twisting Jerry Kennedy's arm, to get him to represent the interests of those three kids in Probate Court—and maybe by so doing to nail Peter Wade.

If you know how to read American English with your ears, you'll know you are dealing with two rare and marvelous chapters. Higgins has perfect pitch; there's not a flat note in them. That is not to say the monologues are simply realistic, they are not literal renditions of what his character would say. If you read slowly and attentively enough you'll realize that Higgins is writing speeches that represent what Royce Whitlock would say and what he would think while saying it, both in his own distinctive native language. But you can analyze these chapters better and more clearly if you also know John Searle's theory of the role of Background in determining the meaning of statements. That permits you to say that what Higgins has done, without ever violating the rhythms of Whitlock's language, is raise to the level of conscious speech the elements of Whitlock's own Background, the things that he has experienced, that give for him color and purpose to the meaning of what he is saying. Simple realism would have him say, forcefully, maybe even elaborately, that he can't stand useless people; only fiercely complicated realism will mount that declaration on the pilings of deeply driven memories of green flies and Civil War monuments, of a child's efforts to make sense of the things adults make a fuss over, stunt drivers and channel swimmers. Simple realism can produce an angry explication of the essential disorderliness of Peter Wade's way of life, but only a complicated realism will produce, apparently effortlessly, supporting accounts of how the disorderliness manifests itself in a gift for sizing up the weaknesses of cops who will take bribes and lawyers who will do anything for money. By the time you have heard what his wife says about him and how she says it, and what he says about the murderous situation he is dealing with and how he thinks while saying it, you have an extraordinarily clear and solid sense of Royce Whitlock's character.

Royce is a hair shirt of a man; a half an hour with him would have you itching all over. Yet he is plainly, and quite credibly, a man you have to respect and admire; he is, in all senses of the term, a good man. He is also a crazy son of a bitch, yet I must report that some of the experiences that are rattling around in his head have been rattling in mine, too. I did not have to do any research to identify Joie Chitwood and His Hell-Drivers, though I never saw them. I, too, saw that newsreel of the grease-covered lady and I can testify that you couldn't see her nipples. I can tell him the name of the nightclub owner—Billy Rose—and I can correct his memory of the swimmer who married Rose. Eleanor Holm wasn't the greased-over nude who swam the channel; she was the one who got thrown off the 1936 Olympic Team by the prudes who ran it because she drank champagne on the boat going over. And while I am at it, I can also remind him that was the Olympics that were staged in Berlin, the ones at which Jesse Owens showed his black heels to the representatives of the Master Race while their Führer looked on in dismay. In other words I am pretty much as crazy as Royce Whitlock is, and so, I trust, are most of the other people who will read *Sandra Nichols Found Dead*, not to mention the man who wrote it.

Careless readers will breeze through these chapters with a smile on their face; careful readers will want to stand up and cheer.

Searle's idea about Background is helpful in dealing with poetry as well as with prose, though I think he had prose in mind when he worked it out. Certainly you have to qualify his assertion that the sentence is the basic unit of meaning when you are dealing with poetry; the shorter, the more intensely lyrical the poem, the stronger the qualification needs to be, for some great, complexly effective lyrics consist of only a single sentence or two. In such highly condensed lyrical statements, a word or a phrase can do the work of whole sentences in bearing the burden of meaning, but then one simply focuses on the Background of words and phrases rather than of sentences. It is still true that the statement underdetermines meaning and that full comprehension of it requires a lively and sensible response to matters that cannot be made explicit. Consider, for an example, Robert Herrick's wonderful lyric, "Upon Julia's Clothes":

> Whenas in silks my Julia goes,
> Then, then, methinks, how sweetly flows
> That liquefaction of her clothes.
>
> Next, when I cast mine eyes, and see
> That brave vibration, each way free,
> O, how that glittering taketh me!

That dazzled me when I first stumbled across it as an eighteen-year-old and it is still dazzling me these many years later. That is to say, it doesn't appear to make much difference whether you're feeling more than you are understanding or understanding more than you're feeling when you read it; either way, it works. On that first occasion I knew very well what he was talking about, for my own response to that two-way vibration was customarily as keen as keen could be, also as oafish. Herrick's, I felt, was keen, too, but he managed it smoothly, deftly, comically, even, which I thought was an enviable achievement. I thought that getting away with using that word "liquefaction" was another enviable achievement. I don't think my delight, which I do remember with surprising clarity, went any deeper into Herrick's artfulness than that. Now, after I-don't-know-how-many encounters with the poem, I understand a lot more about what it means and how it works, but I can't explain how it can remain so *freshly* delightful. Now I recognize and take pleasure in his management of sound and diction. I savor the three perfect rhymes in each stanza and the strong, almost-but-not-quite regular meter; together they give the poem something like an air of childish innocence. In contrast, the "whenas . . . then" structure of the first sentence and the heavily Latinate quality of "liquefaction" smack of an effort to be calmly pedantic, though the second "then" suggests analogical urgency bubbling beneath the surface. The second stanza recognizes the strongly sexual content of his response to that "brave vibration" and quite emphatically—sardonically, even—has no interest in anything either childish or pedantic. The last line, which brings the lyric to such a firm closure that I doubt if any reader finding it at the bottom of a page would ever turn to the next page looking for another stanza, very carefully refuses to characterize just how that "glittering" taketh him and yet permits no doubt whatsoever that it does take him. The contradictions in the poem mock each other, but since they are all perfectly contained by the poem as a whole the mockery is entirely amused, free of any taint of cynicism. At eighteen or at seventy-two, the image of that flowing silken gown glittering as it swings each way free is a joy and a blessing.

I am quite conscious that in formulating even this brief and personal response to "Upon Julia's Clothes" I am indebted to the New Critics—Brooks, Warren, Ransom, et al.—for they taught me and just about everybody else in my generation of academics and the next, and maybe the next after that, most of what we know about how to read a poem as though it were a poem, not a literary document illustrative of something of historical note. Yet I am aware of how I have long since backed off from the manners and methods of the more zealous proponents of the New Criticism that followed in the large footsteps of Brooks, Warren, Ransom, et al. The zealots took a sane insistence on paying attention to what the words in a poem actually mean to warrant a search for what they could be understood to mean; they also converted an insistence on seeing a poem as a work of art with a life of its own into a warrant to ignore the fundamental truth that a poem, like any other work of art, is itself a fragment of the past. I didn't want to have anything to do with wrenching words out of context and arguing from a long-forgotten denotation here and a faintly possible connotation there that some notion that nowhere breaks the surface of the poem is its intended theme; nor did I wish to join the ranks of the historically illiterate and blandly assume that what we think and do is what sensible people have always thought and done. I was even less willing to seize on the modernist interest in symbolism of the original New Critics as a license to go symbol hunting, which I consider one of the more idiotic pursuits known to criticism. Finally, I realized that anything like a zealous approach to the explication of single poems was a disaster in my classes, because it kept generating situations where I was playing the role of the expert and the students were clamming up, unwilling to risk looking bad by venturing opinions of their own. The best of them got sullen; the worst—at least the most objectionable of them—tried to parrot whatever line they thought I was taking.

Backing away, I took to laying more and more emphasis on the Background involved in the poems at hand. That is, after reading John Searle I realize that is what I was doing; at the time, I thought I was just getting my students to approach the poems by way of their own uncertainties about it. More exactly, I kept hammering away at two injunctions: "Read as literally as you can as long as you can," and "Never mind what you don't know, concentrate on what you do know." Those injunctions are not as easy to accept as people might think. Inexperienced students, like inexperienced readers of all kinds, are afraid of writing that seems at all strange, especially, but not exclusively, poems. They are afraid the poems will make them look foolish, and they can't believe that a professor who is telling them to read the first sentence of a *poem* literally isn't trying to make them feel and look foolish. Nor will they, with all the experience they have had taking tests and getting grades, believe that they should not worry about what they don't know. Fear is the great, pernicious foe of understanding. But I am stubborn and most students are finally good-humored enough to play a game, even one that seems silly. Once I could get them to say out loud that Herrick was writing about a girl named Julia wearing a silk dress or something, it was downhill the rest of the way; at least it was with that poem. It took a lot more struggles with a lot more poems to get them to accept the idea that an understanding of a poem has to begin on the literal level; it took even longer to get them to stop worrying about matters they couldn't control—things they didn't even know about—and to concentrate on what they could not only control but enlarge. Only after that, after my students were comfortable in their assurance that they really did understand some things about the poem and convinced that you don't have to know everything about a poem in order to enjoy it, only then did it make sense to go into the deep, logically ordered analysis of the poem's methods and effects that the New Critics called for. To put it more succinctly, I thought that a lot of critics of the period, including some whose work I generally admired, fell into a reductionist trap and tried to base an understanding of a work on an analysis of its component parts before they had an adequate sense of its overall qualities. A poem is a work of art, and its whole is greater than the sum of its parts. That's why you can't approach one with mathematical logic. My spirits would freeze at the thought of using Brooks and Warren's *Understanding Poetry*, brilliant as it unquestionably is, as the text in a freshman course in literature, though a senior-level course might be a very different matter.

Please note that I am only backing away from the New Criticism; I am not trashing it in the fashion of the ideological critics of recent years. They have to trash it because their ideologies cannot endure close analysis of the language necessary to expound them. They can't tolerate John Searle any better because Searle's way of dealing with Background exposes the emptiness of the abstract slogans of an ideology as plainly as close reading does.

The techniques of close reading worked really well only with fairly short lyric poems; with longer poems they didn't help much, perhaps simply because the length of the poems made close reading more burdensome, but probably because they had a much stronger narrative content. Lyric demands close attention and rewards it; narrative asks for and rewards a somewhat looser, dreamier kind of attention. New Criticism served moderately well in dealing with short stories, especially with emphatically modernist ones that seemed to demand explication, but for the most part it seemed to me of little or no help with novels, not even the modernist ones. If it illuminated Henry James's marvelously wrought structures, it missed the melodramatic and comic urgencies of his narratives. It may have helped readers get a grip on *Ulysses*, though I think it did so at the cost of breaking its narrative down into a sequence of lightly connected chapters, but I think it did great damage to Faulkner by over-intellectualizing the novels. Further, it always struck me as being too tightly wrapped, too full of nervous energy to be patient enough to let a novel unfold at its own, frequently slow pace. All of that may be too windy and theoretical, yet this is certainly true: in the years of the New Criticism's ascendancy people who prided themselves on taking literature seriously had trouble taking all but a few emphatically experimental novels seriously.

I am a novel reader. I used to say jokingly that I don't understand ideas very well until I have read about them in a novel; I'm now inclined to think that's no joke. Philosophers, social scientists, politicians, journalists, and so forth tend to give me ideas in their most abstract form, and I can generally manage to get a decent top-of-the-head understanding of them. But novelists give me ideas in the context of the company they keep so that I can learn their real nature and how I might live with them. In other, older, better, less foggy words, novels tell stories, and stories are finally more meaningful than arguments and discourses. Many proper academicians will deny that, if only because they have invested so much of their own lives in mastering logic and the rhetoric of discourse; some have even gone so far as to pin their hopes on the possibilities of artificial intelligence. Roger Penrose is a brilliant mathematician who brings in *The Emperor's New Mind* great quantities of mathematics to bear on the job of demolishing the arguments of the proponents of artificial intelligence; but when he comes to the very end of his book and wishes to complete the demolition—to render unimaginable the will-o'-the-wisp of a computer that is so powerful as to be capable of consciousness—he tells a little science fiction story about the day they activate the 10^{17} logical units of Ultronic, the computer that knows everything. A small boy in the audience is chosen to be the first to pose a question to Ultronic; he wants to know what it feels like to be a computer. Ultronic reports that it can't answer the question, that it can't even understand what the boy is getting at.

That is scarcely a complex story echoing with numerous meanings, but it does something in the way of making meaning that Penrose for all of his intellectual powers can't do in any other way. For a much more powerful bit of storytelling I will turn soon to the second volume of *Don Quixote*, but I think it will help if I approach Cervantes by way of Milan Kundera. Kundera is both a Czech novelist and a French intellectual—that is, he has written seven admirable works of fiction in his native Czech and has made a place for himself among Parisian intellectuals since his emigration from

Czechoslovakia in 1975, writing, in French, a play based on Diderot's *Jacques and His Master*, two nonfiction works, *The Art of the Novel* and *Testaments Betrayed*, and most recently, an eighth novel, *Silence*. The French intellectual in him gives a particularly interesting spin to his novels, especially *The Unbearable Lightness of Being* and *Immortality*, and the Czech novelist weaves together the speculations of the French intellectual so that they have something of the formal intricacy and the specificity of a novel.

Kundera doesn't see the novel as a mere genre for a literary critic to give more or less grudging recognition to, but as the source of some of the most powerful insights of European culture. In *The Art of the Novel*, he gives Cervantes equal credit with Descartes as the founder of the Modern Era. "Indeed, all the great existential themes Heidegger analyzes in *Being and Time* . . . had been unveiled, displayed, illuminated by four centuries of the novel. . . . In its own way, through its own logic, the novel discovered the various dimensions of existence one by one. . . . The novel has accompanied man uninterruptedly and faithfully since the beginning of the Modern Era." Its spirit, Kundera says, is the spirit of complexity, but it is also the spirit of continuity. In fidelity to it he has broken with his former allegiance to the avant-garde, which he now realizes is craven finally in its flattery of the spirit of the time and of the future. Then, he asks, "To what am I attached? To God? Country? The people? The individual? My answer is as ridiculous as it is sincere: I am attached to nothing but the depreciated legacy of Cervantes."[5]

If that smacks a bit too strongly of the French intellectual, consider the passage in his Jerusalem Prize Address in 1985 at Hebrew University in which he develops Flaubert's idea that the novelist is one who seeks to disappear behind his work. Flaubert, he says, renounces the role of public figure for fear that it would endanger his work, making it "a mere appendage to his actions, to his declarations, to his statements of position." Kundera holds that the novelist is nobody's spokesman, he is not even the spokesman for his own ideas. "When Tolstoy sketched the first draft of *Anna Karenina*, Anna was a most unsympathetic woman, and her tragic end was entirely deserved and justified. The final version of the novel is very different, but I do not believe that Tolstoy had revised his moral ideas

5. Milan Kundera, *The Art of the Novel*, 5, 20.

in the meantime; I would say, rather, that in the course of writing, he was listening to another voice than that of his personal moral conviction. He was listening to what I would like to call the wisdom of the novel. Every true novelist listens for that suprapersonal wisdom, which explains why great novels are always a little more intelligent than their authors. Novelists who are more intelligent than their books should go into another line of work."[6] No mere intellectual ever did such a quick, firm job of putting the intellect in its place.

Or better, go on to *Testaments Betrayed,* with its careful, detailed appreciations of the great European novelists, Kafka especially. I will stress just two main points of his discussion of Kafka. First, he shows that Max Brod, Kafka's friend and (in effect) literary executor grossly distorted the public image of Kafka and of his works by publishing a very bad, very sentimental, regrettably popular novel called *The Enchanted Kingdom of Love,* which features a very flattering self-portrait of Brod and an oleaginous portrait of Kafka as "a saint of our time." The pious religiosity and sentimental condescension of the novel were reinforced first by Brod's prefaces to Kafka's hitherto unpublished novels and then by not one but four books of biographical interpretation. "Max Brod," Kundera argues, "created the image of Kafka and that of his work; he created Kafkology at the same time." He defines Kafkology by a tautology: "Kafkology is discourse for Kafkologizing Kafka. For replacing Kafka with the Kafkologized Kafka."[7] Kundera's method for rescuing Kafka from the Kafkologists sounds simple, though in practice it requires some tightly disciplined reading; he reads the novels slowly and literally. By so doing he makes it indisputably clear that they constitute a notably tough-minded kind of comedy about the appalling difficulties of the modern world. He lifts the fog of Kafkology through which for years Americans had to try to read *The Trial, The Castle,* and the other works and shows us in the details of scene after scene a major novelist at work.

Kundera reaches his clearest statement of the rationale for his method of reading novels in the course of correcting a reviewer's

6. Ibid., 158.
7. Milan Kundera, *Testaments Betrayed: An Essay in Nine Parts,* 38, 42.

misapprehension of a scene in one of his own works, *The Book of Laughter and Forgetting*, involving a writer and a professor, both of whom Kundera thought were too impressed with their own brilliance. The reviewer (and a number of other readers) assumed the characters were speaking for Kundera because he did not ridicule them. Kundera concedes he had not made his reservations about the pair obvious; in fact, he had tried to conceal it.

> If I had made their talk ridiculous, by exaggerating its excesses, I would have produced what is called satire. Satire is a thesis art; sure of its own truth, it ridicules what it determines to combat. The novelist's relation to his characters is never satirical; it is ironic. But how does irony, which is by definition discreet, make itself apparent? By the context. . . . Irony means: none of the assertions found in a novel can be taken by itself, each of them stands in a complex and contradictory juxtaposition with other assertions, other situations, other gestures, other ideas, other events. Only a slow reading, twice and many times over, can bring out all the *ironic connections* inside a novel, without which the novel remains uncomprehended.[8]

That statement of rationale comes relatively late in *Testaments Betrayed*, in the eighth of its nine "parts." A gorgeous demonstration of its validity comes earlier, in the fifth part, which he calls "*À la Recherche du Présent Perdu*." The title refers to his idea that the concreteness of the present moment disappears as soon as we try to discuss or analyze it in any way. We cannot discuss the moment, only the memory of the moment, and memory is always vague, abstract, schematic. "Remembering is not the negative of forgetting. Remembering is a form of forgetting." As he sees the evolution of the novel, the need "to resist the loss of the fleeting reality of the present" arose relatively late. Boccaccio and the novelists who came after him accepted memory's way of rendering the past abstractly so fully that they told their stories without concrete scenes, nearly without dialogue, simply concentrating on causal sequences. It wasn't, he thinks, until the beginning of the nineteenth century that the scene became "the *basic* element of the novel's composition." That potentially raised the issue of present, concrete reality, but Balzac and Dostoyevsky led the novel toward a theatrical handling of the scenes. "It was Flaubert ('our most respected, honored

8. Ibid., 202–3.

master,' as Hemingway called him in a letter to Faulkner) who moved the novel away from theatricality" toward "capturing the concreteness of the present," a trend that reached its apogee in James Joyce's *Ulysses*. He notes that Hemingway was particularly obsessed with catching the structure of real conversation, as opposed to the structure of theatrical dialogue; the halting illogicality, the enigmatic absence of explanations, and the repetitions and awkwardness of his dialogues "reveal the characters's obsessions and imbue the conversation with a particular melody. . . . This melodization of dialogue is what is so striking in Hemingway, so entrancing."[9] It is also, I would add, what makes Hemingway so easy to parody and so fiercely hard to equal.

In his first examination of "Hills like White Elephants" at the beginning of part 5, Kundera emphasizes how little we really know about what is going on beyond the bare facts of persons and place—an American man and woman sitting at a table outside the bar of a small railroad station in Spain somewhere between Barcelona and Madrid. It seems certain that they are talking about her having an abortion (the word is never spoken) but we don't know anything about their past or their motivations. She is tense and he is trying, obtusely, ineffectively, to calm her. The story ends with the man, who has had a quick drink while getting their bags, asking "Do you feel better?" "I feel fine," she says. "There's nothing wrong with me. I feel fine."

Kundera observes that the great oddity about this five-page story, which consists almost entirely of banal, disjointed dialogue, is that it permits us to imagine any number of radically different stories implicit in it and similarly permits us to imagine the nature of the characters in any number of different ways. The closest the story comes to giving us a conventional revelation of their natures is when the girl says that the hills look like white elephants.

> "I've never seen one," the man drank his beer.
> "No, you wouldn't have."
> "I might have," the man said. "Just because you say I wouldn't have doesn't prove anything."

She comes back to the metaphor a couple of pages later after the man protests,

9. Ibid., 128–30, 136–37.

"You know I love you."

"I know. But if I do it, then it will be nice again if I say things are like white elephants, and you'll like it?"

"I'll love it. I love it now but I just can't think about it. You know how I get when I worry."

That's scarcely the material for an incisive characterization. Very deliberately—indeed, by rendering with patient skill the results of much disciplined observation of the conversation of unhappy lovers—Hemingway has given us a story that is simultaneously remarkably concrete and extremely abstract. Because it is that way, because it is so calmly exact about the specifics of a commonplace exchange of remarks, "Hills like White Elephants" opens up to any and all of us so that we can for once imagine a present moment and thereby know a little more about life "in our time" (to use the title of his first, almost revolutionary, collection of stories). To blur that abstractness, to account for the dialogue by settling on a single story involving neatly defined characters, would be the literary equivalent of repainting Picasso's portrait of those "Demoiselles d'Avignon" to get rid of the cubist distortions. Or, to use the example Kundera develops at some length, the equivalent of improving one of Janáček's operas by drowning out with conventionally "operatic" orchestrations the strange new melodies that Janáček had learned how to create through years of patiently rendering in musical notation the melody in the remarks he overheard on the sidewalks of Prague.

In such matters you can trust a bad biographer to do a thorough job of defacing the work of art, because a bad biographer, by definition, has the silly notion that a nice, simple, one-to-one relationship exists between a novelist's life and his work, and the even sillier notion that the biographer is superior to the novelist whose life he is so blithely analyzing. Jeffrey Meyers, who has the necessary qualifications, does a particularly egregious job of "explaining" the story in his biography of Hemingway; Kundera takes after him, hatchet in hand. Meyers begins, Kundera says, by observing that the story "may . . . portray Hemingway's response to Hadley's [his first wife's] second pregnancy." (The cognoscenti may wish to pause to savor that brief statement: the politely feigned uncertainty of *may*, the unpretentious academic elegance of *portray*, and the biographical precision of Hadley's *second* pregnancy.) In Meyers's reduction of Hemingway's beautifully abstract story into a trite moral tale safe for publication in even the most politically correct of journals, the woman is a sweetly natural lover of babies who is being bullied into having an abortion by an abominably egotistical, grossly insensitive male—that is, she is a lovely modern American woman and he is the chauvinist pig that everybody these days knows Ernest Hemingway to have been. "The comparison of hills with white elephants—imaginary animals that represent useless items, like the unwanted baby, is crucial to the meaning," says Meyers. Kundera adds,

> the comparison, a bit forced, of elephants with unwanted babies is not Hemingway's but the professor's; it is needed to set up the sentimental interpretation of the story. "The simile becomes a focus of contention and establishes an opposition between the imaginative woman, who is moved by the landscape, and the literal-minded man, who refuses to sympathize with her point of view. . . . The theme of the story evolves from a series of polarities: natural v. unnatural, instinctive v. rational, reflective v. talkative, vital v. morbid." The professor's intention becomes clear: to make the woman the morally positive pole, the man the morally negative pole.

And so it goes for three and a half acid-dipped pages, Meyers twisting this way and that in order to make the story say what he knows it should say, and Kundera italicizing the fact that nothing in the story supports Meyers's fatuous reading. Kundera finally summarizes the summary, driving his hatchet still deeper into the professor's skull. He concludes that "this other story" (the one Meyers has invented to replace Hemingway's) "is absolutely flat and all clichés; nevertheless, because it is compared successively with Dostoyevsky, Kafka, the Bible, and Shakespeare . . . it retains its status as a great work and therefore, despite its author's moral poverty, justifies the professor's interest in it."[10]

Kundera commented, as I noted earlier, that Tolstoy's plan for *Anna Karenina* changed as he wrote it because he found that he had to stop heeding his own personal moral conviction and listen to "the wisdom of the novel," which is "a suprapersonal wisdom." "Great novels," Kundera observed, "are always a little more intelli-

10. Jeffrey Meyers, *Hemingway, a Biography*, 196–97; Kundera, *Testaments*, 142–45.

gent than their authors."[11] I think we could broaden that a little and say that great stories are always a little more intelligent than their tellers: "Hills like White Elephants" is more intelligent than Ernest Hemingway in the very same way that *Anna Karenina* is more intelligent than Leo Tolstoy. That creates a special difficulty for critics: whatever wisdom they possess is every bit as personal as writers', and it would seem to follow that great stories are always a little more intelligent than critics, too. But if their public function is to demonstrate high literary intelligence, as a lot of people believe, how can critics be expected to defer to the intelligence of mere stories? It's all right for writers to appear sort of dopey—witness William Faulkner's performances as a hunting, drinking fellow who just happened to know a lot of stories about people in his neck of the woods—but how can an assistant professor at a good university expect to get tenure if he keeps denigrating his own intelligence? It can be done, as a lot of scholars and critics who modestly claim only to be very lucky have shown, but it's hard; it goes against the grain of anybody who has painstakingly learned to jump the hurdles in graduate school, let alone of anybody sharp enough to win status as a French intellectual after emigrating from Czechoslovakia. Kundera's method is perfect: he reads as literally as he can as long as he can; he submits to the necessity to read accurately before starting to float ideas about the work at hand. Unlike bad biographers and foolish critics, Kundera insists on observing *exactly* what happens in *The Castle* before formulating any theories about its meaning and on reading one sentence after another, not once but several times over, before trying to think very much about the significance of "Hills like White Elephants." That slow, patient, unflashy reading—that avoidance of interpretation—is the essential discipline for any critic of novels.

The essential study for any such critic—for anyone, really, who wants to claim to be decently educated—is *Don Quixote,* for it constitutes the finest possible demonstration of the power of story and of the art of storytelling. For my purposes here a single example from it will do. It comes from the prologue to part 2 as translated by Samuel Putnam. (I will take up later the argument for reading novels in translation; I will just observe here that the novel is in

11. Kundera, *Testaments,* 158.

point of well-founded fact an international form and that translations of part 1 of *Don Quixote* became extremely popular in England
and throughout Europe almost as soon as it was published in 1605.)

In 1614 one who signed himself Alonso Fernandez de Avellaneda published a book that claimed to be a sequel to part 1 and
thereby took his place among the great damned fools of all time.
Nobody but a fool would be fat-headed enough to think that he
could match the lovely subtleties of Cervantes's book, and only a
damned fool would then go out of his way to mock Cervantes for
his crippled left hand, the result of wounds suffered while fighting
with notable bravery in Spain's greatest naval triumph. Apparently
rumor or wishful thinking had persuaded Avellaneda that it
was safe to carry on in such fashion, for it had been nine years since
part 1 was published and Cervantes was close to fifty-eight at that
time. But Cervantes was very much alive and deep into the writing
of his own authentic sequel to part 1. In his prologue to part 2,
which was published in 1615, he asked his readers to convey a message to Avellaneda:

> If you by chance should come to know him, tell him on my behalf that
> I do not hold it against him; for I know what temptations the devil has
> to offer, one of the greatest of which consists in putting it into a man's
> head that he can write a book and have it printed and thereby achieve
> as much fame as he does money and acquire as much money as he
> does fame; in confirmation of which I would have you, in your own
> witty and charming manner, tell him this tale.
>
> There was in Seville a certain madman whose madness assumed
> one of the drollest forms that was ever seen in this world. Taking a
> hollow reed sharpened at one end, he would catch a dog in the street
> or somewhere else; and, holding one of the animal's legs with his foot
> and raising the other with his hand, he would fit his rod as best he
> could in a certain part, after which he would blow the dog up, round
> as a ball. When he had it in this condition he would give it a couple of
> slaps on the belly and let it go, remarking to the bystanders, of whom
> there were always plenty, "Do your worships think, then, it is so easy
> a thing to inflate a dog?" So you might ask, "Does your Grace think
> that it is so easy a thing to write a book?"[12]

Now, *that* is a demonstration of the storyteller's art! It bears the
hallmark of the true, sterling article: it reaches meanings that could

---

12. Miguel de Cervantes, *The Ingenious Gentleman Don Quixote de la Mancha*,
506.

neither be reached nor unraveled by a logical, social-scientific, analytical mind operating in its customary way. That mind operates by means of reducing things (of whatever sort) to their component parts and then organizing the parts according to some hierarchical order. It sorts things out and then deals first with this, then with that; just the opposite of the storytelling mind, which scoops up possibilities, packs them together as though it were making mental snowballs, and tosses them into the air for the rest of us to admire or not admire, as we wish.

Consider what the problem was here: Cervantes wanted to reprove a fool for attempting to steal his work and his fame, and to do so vigorously enough that neither he nor anyone else will ever again be tempted to try that stunt. We have plenty of illustrations of how a strong analytical mind would deal with such a problem; the "Letters" section of the *New York Review of Books* and other periodicals for intellectuals are full of them. I have seen many good people from the various arts and sciences do a skillful job of telling fools off, but I have never seen anybody do what Cervantes does in this bit of a story—define in one breath both the foolishness of the fool and the foolishness of the fame the fool is trying to steal from him. If that's a clumsy way of stating the matter, my excuse is that the story stoutly resists analytical explanation. Let me try again. A letter-writing analyst would have no trouble blistering the fool for his incompetent thievery, but he would have difficulty maintaining an urbane tone and he is not at all likely to frame the reproof in precisely the sort of statement the fool was incompetent to duplicate. I don't think there is a ghost of a chance he would manage to suggest at the same time that the fool was handicapped not only by incompetence but also by the sort of false dignity that would keep him from identifying in any important way with a madman who went around blowing air up the rectal systems of stray dogs. Put that way, one can hardly blame the fool for his reluctance, yet that indeed is the way Cervantes put it. He did identify with a madman who thought he was a knight errant; he went further (this is the main business of part 2) and identified also with a fat peasant who had served so faithfully as "squire" to the "knight" as to become for many practical purposes indistinguishable from him. That is to say, Cervantes submitted to the story given to him to tell; a novelist dare not be too proud, too refined to do that. In Kundera's terms, he acknowledged that the novel is more intelligent than the novelist. People with analytical minds cannot manage that sort of submission, for, mind you, it is breathtaking.

Avellaneda, whose mind very possibly wasn't worth much for analytical purposes either, couldn't do it. It is amusing to imagine the expressions that must have passed over Avellaneda's face as he listened to the story told in the "witty and charming manner" of one of Cervantes's readers (who no doubt was glad to volunteer for the job). Retell the story today to some proudly serious possessors of analytical minds, as I have done on more than one occasion, and you will see some fine samples of nose-wrinkled disgust. "Blowing air up a dog's rectum? Good God!" Their major reason for so reacting, very probably the only one that they would think to give, is that the image is both extremely crude and offensively callous with respect to poor madmen and to helpless animals; they wouldn't want to have anything to do with such a matter, not even in their thoughts. Yet Cervantes, who knew people, was of the opinion that there would always be plenty of bystanders; in twentieth-century America as in seventeenth-century Spain the crowd would include a lot of respectable people, probably all of the ones who were lucky enough to come along at the right time. But I strongly suspect that underneath that respectable reason for their revulsion runs a line of thought they would rather not have to lift up for inspection. Cervantes was, as all even faintly literate people know today, a great artist who won fame and money in his own time and immortality after; that is, he possessed in very large measure status that all proudly serious analytical types would give anything to achieve. Cervantes knew that, too, for he knew "what temptations the devil has to offer." Yet the story puts the work that wins such status on a level with a madman's enterprise in inflating dogs; that's more than any serious scholar/scientist should have to listen to. And to make bad matters worse, most of those Serious people really do think it is easy to write a novel—at least a lot easier than it is to write a Serious book. That makes the madman smarter than they are? Impossible!

Those of us, however, who are natural-born novel-readers, don't have to analyze that story and we don't have to be offended by it because we long ago made our peace with stories. We not only

don't mind that the story is more intelligent than we are, we are re-
lieved to be free to wallow in it to our heart's delight, analytical dignity be damned.

Does your Grace think that it is so easy a thing to write a novel,
or even to read one?

5

In Praise of Translations

Purists sniff in disdain at the thought of studying important works of literature in translation. They take the position that a translation can give only a feeble, distorted version of a great work and hold that if you want to know, say, *Don Quixote,* you have to read it in the original Spanish. As John McCormick, a professor of comparative literature with a command of several languages, put it in a review of Burton Raffel's new translation of *Don Quixote,* "anyone with a decent command of Spanish can read the novel without major difficulty, and anyone really wanting to read Cervantes, not Raffel, will do so." There are defects in that position, though you have to respect the one-upmanship with which he presents it. Purists generally admit that Americans tend to assume that they need no language other than English, but they will not stoop to condoning such weakness. In McCormick's words, "we Americans would seem either arrogant in that assumption, perpetrators of linguistic nationalism, or victims of linguistic *pudor,* shame at being tongue-tied and inarticulate in another language."[1] Since all scholars in a field as huge and as complex as literature must live with the guilt of not knowing large amounts of important material, the timid majority will join in the deploring of translations and resign themselves to teaching only works that their lamentably monolingual students can read, carefully dumping the blame on students, who are not there to defend themselves. Only the brass-bound will join me in replying that linguistic nationalism is one of the few offenses I haven't perpetrated and that I am not a victim of linguistic *pudor* because it doesn't occur in the lingo I grew up in.

The ploys and counterploys of one-upmanship aside, academic

1. John McCormick, "Down with Translation," lxix, lxx.

84

disdain for literature in translation is wrong both in theory and in practical fact, though it is of course correct in impossible ideal. Ideally, I would read every work I want to read in its original language and with the easy accuracy of an educated native speaker of that language. No translator, no matter how gifted and industrious, can possibly duplicate in a second language what an artist has created in his own language; for all practical purposes nothing in one language can be exactly duplicated in another. Yet that doesn't matter nearly as much as it would seem to because for all such practical purposes nothing in the experience of one person can be duplicated in the experience of another. All our realities are individual and any accounts we give of them are approximate, no matter what language we may be using. All languages, as I argued in earlier chapters, are designed to let us live with our uncertainties and approximations. Literary criticism has to begin with the knowledge that no two people, however fluent they may be in a language, can ever read the same literary work in the same way; inserting a competent translation into the process will not necessarily make matters much worse.

Let me come at this in a different way. One work of literature in a foreign language that I had many excellent reasons for thinking I needed to know was—naturally, inevitably—*Don Quixote*. I couldn't read Spanish and I couldn't afford the time to learn how; a translation was my only hope. On my first try I read Shelton's famous seventeenth-century version; though it was hard going, in places at least I could make out some of what Henry Fielding found so exciting in it. I think (by now I cannot be at all sure) that I dipped into some other rather feeble translations before I got to J. M. Cohen's quite readable one in Penguin's series of great works in translation. That was in the mid-fifties; a decade or so later I read, and promptly wished I were capable of memorizing, Samuel Putnam's translation. I have looked into some other translations that I thought were competent, though not in a class with Putnam's. I still have not, by Professor McCormick's standard, read Cervantes's *Don Quixote*, but by practicing something like the navigator's art of triangulation I think I have located that very great work accurately enough to permit me to savor its vision and understand its huge influence on nearly all subsequent works of comic art. (I might add that I did it all on my own, for the highly reputable institutions in which I did my undergraduate and graduate work shied away from the shoddy business of studying works of literature in translation.)

Purists don't seem to understand that good readers commonly, almost routinely, check one translation against another before settling on the one they want generally to rely on; Professor McCormick appears so little interested in the variety of translations available that he makes no reference to Samuel Putnam's and treats J. M. Cohen's, which I think is slightly pedestrian, as the standard for English versions of *Don Quixote*. Offhand, I cannot think of a single instance of a classic work from another language that I have not been able to read in at least two different translations; when it comes to the works of great dramatists such as Ibsen and Chekhov, like everybody else who wants to understand them I am familiar with four or five or more translations of the key plays. However, you don't have to have comparisons available to make a reasonably sound judgment of a given translation. Molière is a special case: in the forties and fifties I knew he was a huge influence on English comic dramatists from Wycherly to Shaw, but I couldn't find a translation that gave me even a glimpse of his power until Richard Wilbur's translations of *The Misanthrope* and *Tartuffe* came out. I like Wilbur's poetry very much, but his translations of Molière are his ticket of admission to immortality. Jaroslav Hašek's *The Good Soldier Švejk* is another interesting case in point. I had been told by Czech-reading friends that it was a marvelous comic novel, but the only English translation of it that was then available was absolutely unreadable—weirdly genteel and euphemistic. A few years later, in the mid-seventies, Cecil Parrott's new translation became available in this country; I read it with great delight. It's not perfect, for though Parrott is not genteel he flinches, in the opinion of those who can judge, from the cheerful, freewheeling obscenity of the original. We need a translator untouched by Puritanism, a Henry Miller who can read Czech, and they are in exceedingly short supply. Still, Parrott has made it possible for me to savor a lot of the joy of one of the great works of comic literature; none of my colleagues who disdain translations have the faintest notion of what it is like.

Purists almost always try to shame us one book and one language at a time; Professor McCormick thinks it shabby of us not to learn Spanish in order to read *Don Quixote* in the original just as another purist scorns us for not learning French in order to read *Madame Bovary* and a third one shakes a finger at us for not learning German in order to read Goethe. They rarely hold up all three books and all three languages at the same time; even the polylingual can see that would be too discouraging. But in point of fact even three at a time would be too few. *The Iliad, The Odyssey,* and a generous sampling of the Greek tragedies are necessary elements in a decent literary education; so, too, are the Latin poets and Dante. Anyone who gets interested in drama is going to need to know plays that were originally written in Greek, Latin, Italian, French, Spanish, German, Norwegian, and one or more Central European languages; and the serious pursuit of the novel is at least as polyglot. I have never happened to hear a purist so pure as to complain about those who don't have a reading knowledge of Russian, but how can anybody who hasn't read Tolstoy and Dostoyevsky claim to know modern literature?

The simple impure truth of the matter is that translations are necessary to the study of literature and that both the novel and drama, perhaps especially the novel, are for both their practitioners and their readers international forms. Georges Simenon, to take a spectacular example, wrote more than 250 short novels in French, a great many of them showing a clear debt to Dostoyevsky, whose novels he read in translation. All of Simenon's novels have been translated into other languages; by the last count I heard, at least one Simenon has been translated into one or more of some sixty different languages. Ernest Hemingway, who worked so hard to perfect a crystalline kind of American English, has been, even in translation, a major influence on novelists in every language of Europe, and very possibly of Asia, India, and Africa, too.

Lyric poetry would seem to be a different matter, for when it is at all good it is tightly and deeply embedded in its own language. Single words and phrases count for so much in a good line of poetry and the rhythms and sounds of groups of lines are so powerful that the chances of finding anything but approximate equivalents in another language seem faint. We can't reasonably expect to have good translations generally available; we have to hope that one of our own gifted poets will be so moved by the foreign poem as to write a poem of his own in response to it. Yet all that being said and due acknowledgment given to Professor McCormick's reference to Joseph

Brodsky, who "tended to throw up his hands . . . at his own efforts to translate his own Russian into English,"[2] one has to acknowledge that Czeslaw Milosz, who is by common consent one of the great poets of the Polish language, is by virtue of the translations of his own work that he has "coauthored" with native-born speakers of English one of the best American poets of recent decades. Some very good contemporary American poets—W. S. Merwin and Gary Snyder, to name two that come promptly to mind—have done interesting work in the form of translations of European and Asian poetry; and some of our major poets have flourished in translation—Whitman, perhaps especially in German, and Poe, famously in French. Perhaps it ought to be impossible to translate a good lyric poem, but in point of fact it has been done and done well on some number of occasions and with some variety of poems.

None of this will come as a surprise to anyone who is familiar with John Searle's theory of the role of Background in clarifying sentences, which always—of necessity—leave their meanings underdetermined. An outsider may think that translators work word-by-word; even translators may think 'so when they are plowing through difficult passages racking their minds for equivalents to words and phrases in the original. But in truth they are translating sentence-by-sentence or even passage-by-passage, for translators are readers before they are translators and like other readers they almost automatically bring what they know of both the local and deep Background to bear on the literal meaning of the words, sentences, and paragraphs in order to make sense of them.

If you'd rather avoid Searle's technical term *Background,* you could think of it as a matter of putting statements in appropriate and necessary contexts. Nothing makes very much sense out of context; the richer the context a writer and a reader can create for a given statement, the more fully it will be understood. A story, whether it's embedded in a novel, a drama, or an epic poem, is a very powerful device for creating contexts for statements; if the translator gets the story right then the reader will have the key to understanding the statements, even in a relatively rough translation.

Milan Kundera offers a special, comically tangled illustration of these matters. In *Testaments Betrayed,* his impassioned account of

2. Ibid., lxix.

how the sentimentalizing views of Franz Kafka's friend, literary executor, and biographer, Max Brod, has enforced on the public a distorted view of Kafka's novels slides into a diatribe first on Kafka's French translators and then by extension on translators in general. He concentrates on French translations of the sentence in the third chapter of *The Castle* where Kafka describes the coition of K. and Frieda, quoting the versions in Alexandre Vialatte's 1938 translation, Claud David's correction of Vialatte in the 1976 publication of Kafka's novels in the Pléiade series, and Bernard Lortholary's wholly new translation in 1984. For contrast he quotes the sentence in the original German and offers his own exact French translation of it. "The entire sentence," he says, "is one long metaphor. Nothing requires more exactness from a translator than the translation of a metaphor. That is where we glimpse the core of an author's poetic originality."[3] All three of the translators botch the sentence's metaphorical quality, apparently because they either cannot or will not grasp the special quality of what Kundera calls Kafka's "existential or phenomenological" metaphors; his own exact translation of the sentence comes much closer to doing justice to its distinctive power. To this point Kundera seems to be giving us interesting, original criticism, but he goes on to use the three versions as examples of what he thinks are the twin fundamental weaknesses of translators: their inability to resist the urge to replace the author's word with a synonym ("the synonymizing reflex") and their desire to demonstrate the richness of their own vocabularies. And that leads him into lecturing translators in general: their supreme authority should be the author's personal style, not the conventional version of "good" style in the translator's own language.

There are difficulties here. First, his attack on Brod's grossly sentimental version of Kafka is a bit old hat. When I first read Kafka in college in the forties many American and English critics probably were busy following Brod's lead in "Kafkologizing Kafka" (to use Kundera's charmingly dotty term), but in recent decades our critics have come a long way towards understanding the tough-minded humor of his novels and stories. (For example, in the introduction to *The Castle* that he wrote in 1992, Irving Howe observed among a number of other items in a list of Kafka's basic literary methods that

3. Kundera, *Testaments,* 104.

his "fiction is rich in comedy, often in a biting, desperate farce.")[4] Second, an American or English reader will be taken aback by the virulence of Kundera's attack on translators of *The Castle* when he goes to check the translation he himself is accustomed to reading, the one published in 1930 by Willa and Edwin Muir, and finds that in all essential respects it is equal to the "exact translation" that Kundera made in order to correct the three defective French translations. Here, Kundera appears to be sharing in the remarkable chauvinism of French intellectuals who freely make sweeping generalizations on the basis of a very few French examples—the rest of the world, perhaps especially the English-speaking part, doesn't quite exist for them. When he goes on to pontificate about the weaknesses of translators it never seems to occur to him that he is analyzing the qualities of poor translators; it's as though he has never heard of—or doesn't want to admit hearing of—a good translator.

Kundera has had his troubles with translations of his own novels, especially with the English translation of *The Joke*. The "definitive version," published in 1992, is the *fifth* English version to come out since 1969. The first three are variations on a translation by David Hamblyn and Oliver Stallybrass. The first one, published in 1969 by Macdonald in London, is, by all accounts, a garbled mess; the second, by Coward-McCann in New York, later in 1969, claimed to be an improvement, though it is plainly, confusingly incomplete; and the third, published by Penguin in 1970, is more nearly complete but no less inept. At that time Kundera was at the mercy of publishers, for he couldn't leave Czechoslovakia to come protest in person and his letters had little effect. By the early eighties he was living in France and was so pleased, he says, to have his American publisher (Harper and Row by this time) propose a new translation by Michael Henry Heim that he didn't bother to check it with the care he generally gives to the French, Italian, German, and English translations of his novels. (Central European novelists are, of necessity, a polylingual lot.) About ten years later, when his editor, Aaron Asher, proposed republishing *The Joke*, he decided he should take a careful look at the translation and was so horrified by what he found that he persuaded Asher to let him do his own

4. Irving Howe, introduction to *The Castle*, xix.

thorough revision of it. Thus, readers of the novel should now hold out for the "Definitive Version Fully Revised by the Author."

It is indeed a thorough revision and certainly a skillful one: Kundera has brushed up the prose on, I think, nearly every page, doing the things with words and images that only real writers can do. Heim is a competent, hardworking reader and translator, but he doesn't seem to be a real writer. His sentences march sturdily along, but they don't leap and dance. Nonetheless, I must report that Kundera's improvements, interesting and even impressive as they are, do not seem to make a huge difference, certainly nothing like the difference between Heim's version and the first one. Perhaps if I were just starting out with the novel I might be more appreciative of the definitive version, but I read and reread Heim's version of *The Joke* and taught it in class and knew that I was dealing with a first-class novel. Indeed, it prompted me to read all of Kundera's other novels, including *The Book of Laughter and Forgetting* and, later, *The Unbearable Lightness of Being*, both of which were translated by Heim. (I had a lot of company in my enthusiasm; the publication in 1982 of Heim's version seems to have had the effect of fixing Kundera's American reputation as a major writer.) I have to conclude that Heim's translation, unpolished as it might seem, got the story of *The Joke* right and was reasonably alert to matters of Background, and thereby made it possible for poor monolinguals like me to see something of Kundera's Czech artistry.

A reader may come away from this part of *Testaments Betrayed* thinking Kundera looks a bit foolish, but the last laugh belongs to Kundera for his exasperation with bad translations leads him directly into his brilliantly literal reading of "Hills like White Elephants" and on into the most useful exposition I have found of the art of reading a novel. That art applies to the reading of any novel, in or out of translation. Read Parrott's translation of *The Good Soldier Švejk* that way and I don't see how you can avoid realizing that you are dealing with a great, odd work of comic art even while recognizing that the translation may be a bit off. Reading Heim's translation of *The Joke* with that kind of care sent me on to read over the next few months everything of Kundera's then in print. Those other novels, though translated by various hands, created a context that enabled me to get a firmer and firmer sense of what Kundera himself was doing. The truism applies: the best commentary on any given work by a writer is always the rest of that writer's work.

For the habitual reader one book or one writer has a happy way of leading on to other books and other writers. (It's a shame that occasional readers don't trust that process of half-accidental accretion of knowledge instead of begging us habituals for reading lists; they would learn more and have a lot more fun that way. They would also have a chance to become habituals themselves.) Having read *The Good Soldier* and Kundera's first several novels and having seen the distinctively funny and engaging films that Milos Forman made in Czechoslovakia before he immigrated to Hollywood, *Black Peter, Loves of a Blonde,* and *Fireman's Ball,* I kept an eye out for other novels and other films by Kundera's and Forman's Czech contemporaries. I don't think that Forman had very many peers in—or even out of—Czechoslovakia, but Kundera was one of a number of extremely interesting postwar Czech novelists. Jiří Weil (*Life with a Star*), Ivan Klíma (*Love and Garbage* and others), and Bohumil Hrabal (*Closely Watched Trains, I Served the King of England,* and others) are three of that company that I am particularly glad to have made my way to—with the necessary assistance, of course, of good translators such as Paul Wilson, Edith Pargeter, and Ewald Osers.

My great find, though, was Josef Skvorecky. It's not as though he was anything like an obscure writer—he was hugely popular in Czechoslovakia and had the respect of good critics throughout Europe—but he was only dimly recognized in this country when I started to catch up with his work sometime in the eighties. Nobody likes to believe me when I say this, but I strongly suspect the trouble was his name. Few Americans can get their tongue around a name that begins *Skv-* and most are embarrassed to make mistakes in front of librarians and clerks in bookstores. Seeing a baffling Czech diacritical mark over the *S*, the one that looks like an upside-down version of the caret, and an apparently unnecessary stress mark over the *y*, only makes matters worse. Since I am case-hardened by years of blithely mispronouncing unpronounceable names to help ease my students into discussing novels I was making them read, it didn't bother me to tell a clerk in Border's in Ann Arbor that I wanted to find a mystery novel about a Lieutenant Somebody-or-Other by a writer whose name I couldn't pronounce though I remembered it began with an S. The novel was *The Mournful*

Demeanour of Lieutenant Boruvka. Having seen a short review some-where suggesting that it was in the tradition of Simenon's Maigret stories, I thought it might be fun; it was that and much more, even though I still couldn't pronounce the writer's name. I am still botch-ing the Czech pronunciation—it's supposed to be something like "Shkvoretsky"—but I have read and reread all of his books that are available in English and I will gladly testify that he is an important novelist, calling him Joseph Skretsy all the while.

Certainly for me he is a much better novelist than most of the ones that I was supposed to have read and admired in the last twenty years or so. Saul Bellow has won so many prizes and deco-rations that his novels could be stamped "Certified U.S. Prime," but I thought they went downhill after *Augie March,* and I largely gave up on them after *Mr. Sammler's Planet.* They struck me as smacking too much of the University of Chicago with its reverence for Great Books and too little of the boisterous, complicated city of Chicago. I couldn't go the route with John Updike, either; his prose style, his eroticism, and his religiosity are all too fancy for me. After the self-conscious artfulness of Bellow and Updike, and of a number of other much admired novelists who might as well remain nameless on the grounds that taking potshots at writers is a graceless busi-ness, Skvorecky's way of hiding his artfulness behind a mask of or-dinary dopiness was a welcome change; it came as an invitation to participate in whatever thinking had to be done, not just sit back and admire the thinking of a real professional. By now I am long past any sense of reading Skvorecky to fill in a background, a con-text. He is in the foreground, a big writer whose work interacts in highly enlightening ways not only with other Czech writers but with big writers everywhere, especially with the big American writers.

Skvorecky was born in a small town called Nachod on the north-eastern border of Bohemia in the westernmost part of Czechoslova-kia, yet he cut his teeth as an artist reading American novels and mystery stories and spent five or six years in his childhood seeing a movie every day and two on Sunday. As a young man he tried hard to make a jazz saxophonist of himself and later helped to scratch out a living by translating Chandler, Hemingway, Faulkner, and others. That practically makes him an American. Or if that is claim-ing too much, it does mean that he was peculiarly well situated for demonstrating the potent implications of certain American ideas and attitudes when they are translated, so to speak, into Czech. Take the matter of realism in the novel. Anyone who came of age reading American fiction of the twenties and thirties simply knows that a novel ought to deal with the lives that people actually live in our time and ought to do so in the language they actually use, without any trace of condescension. That's the polar opposite of Socialist realism, which deals in suitably elevated language with the lives people ought to or maybe someday will live in a flawless, Soviet-loving state. Skvorecky wrote his first novel, *The Cowards*, in 1948–1949 when the Communists were just taking over in Czechoslovakia and beginning to impose Moscow's idea of Socialist realism on all writers. He has said that he was making a conscious effort to produce a piece of "magic realism"; the term came from the Czech poet Josef Hora, but the concept came from Hawthorne. He was trying to re-create events in his past life so that they would return to him, in Hawthorne's phrase, "etherealized by distance." Specifically, he wrote about the last week of the war, May 4th to May 11th, 1945, as he and his friends experienced it in Nachod and called it *The Cowards* because he and they were too sane and too decent to be anything like the heroes of conventional wartime melodramas; chasing girls and playing jazz was their speed, not fighting wars. He used three epigraphs: one was from Romain Rolland on how the artist creates his work out of the substance of his times; another was from Mezz Mezzrow on how jazz was a revolution simmering in Chicago in the twenties; and the third was Hemingway's deceptively simple statement that "a writer's job is to tell the truth." Nothing like that was going to get published in Czechoslovakia in 1949. Even a decade later, with Stalin safely dead for six years, the decision to publish *The Cowards* cost a number of editors their jobs at the state publishing house and got Skvorecky fired from the staff of the periodical *World Literature*. Truth-telling of the sort that Hemingway and the great jazz musicians had in mind was, is, and always will be intolerable to ideologues everywhere, no matter what particular prescription for perfection they are peddling.

Readers full of ordinary imperfections are a different matter. In a very few years and despite the foot-dragging of authorities, *The Cowards* sold over a hundred thousand copies. It's hard for me to be certain why it was so popular, but its freedom from the formulas of officially approved fiction and its celebration of ordinary people living in a very ordinary town must have been appealing. Skvorecky reports with pleasure that in the years following its publication a surprising number of Czech babies were named after its narrator, Danny Smiricky. Apparently the most startling aspect of *The Cowards* was its free use of slang in the dialogue and its use of spoken Czech, rather than literary Czech, in the narrative. An American reader needs to be told about that, for in Jeanne Němcová's translation it's simply a skillfully informal piece of seemingly autobiographical fiction, a kind of novel we have long since grown comfortable with. To touch again on the argument I was making in Chapter 1, our inheritance from Mark Twain, the American tradition of a heavy vernacular influence on prose style is more important, more meaningful than contemporary criticism has been prepared to admit. A comment in the *New York Review of Books* by J. M. Coetzee is representative, even though Coetzee is himself a novelist and ought to know better: "Skvorecky is not a great prose artist. By comparison with his contemporary Milan Kundera, whose language is masterly in its elegance and lucidity, Skvorecky is an honest journeyman."[5]

Kundera himself would not denigrate Skvorecky's work. He has been consistently generous in his praise of the novels as they have appeared and in a comment in his introduction to the French edition of *The Miracle Game,* one that Coetzee quotes from, apparently without fully understanding it, he argues that in *The Miracle Game,* as in *The Cowards,* written twenty-five years earlier, Skvorecky displays a "special way of viewing history from underneath. . . . The humour is coarse, in the tradition of Jaroslav Hašek. There's an extraordinary gift for anecdote, and a mistrust of ideology and the myths of history. Little inclination for the preciousness of modernist prose, a simplicity verging on the provocative, in spite of a very refined literary culture. And finally . . . an anti-revolutionary spirit."[6] That could nearly serve as a generic description of the Mark Twain tradition in fiction. Kundera, it should be noted, sees these important qualities in the original Czech versions of the novels; we can see them just as clearly (with a little prompting from Kundera)

5. J. M. Coetzee, "Only in Amerika," 14.
6. Milan Kundera, "Preface to the French Edition of *Mirakl (The Miracle Game),*" 29.

in the English versions. And we who have grown up embedded in the Twain tradition should readily understand, as Coetzee, who is South African, does not or cannot, that you can't achieve such intellectual insights without first developing a prose style that is soaked in the language of common talk.

I don't want to beat too hard on Coetzee—his views are representative; the woods are full of critics who are blandly dismissive of prose and humor of a Twainian sort—but he is exactly, even precisely, wrong in terming the author of *The Cowards* a mere journeyman. I might even argue that he is wrong in comparing him unfavorably to Kundera, whose writing he finds "masterly in its elegance and lucidity." The older Kundera gets the more fully he becomes a French intellectual and the more arid, I think, his fiction becomes; his two most recent novels, *Immortality* and *Silence*, are brilliant discourses, but they lack the imaginative force of *The Joke* and *The Book of Laughter and Forgetting*. There is no drying out in Skvorecky's novels, only a deepening understanding and a growing reach; past seventy, he is still engrossed in novels as the only adequate way of expressing his vision.

Skvorecky (in an essay he wrote for *Contemporary Authors: Autobiography Series* and reprinted in *Talkin' Moscow Blues*) divides, somewhat impishly, the credit for his discovery of the power of the vernacular between Ernest Hemingway and a shopgirl who called herself Maggie. In tribute to her he wrote a novel called *The Nylon Age* that plainly couldn't be submitted for publication, not in the Czechoslovakia of 1954. Two years later he wrote another novel called *The End of the Nylon Age* that he didn't think was so offensive to official tastes and standards. "It was quickly seized," he says, "by the censors and banned before publication as 'pornography,' due to my use of the word 'bosom' to describe a woman's (certainly not bare) breasts. When I suggested to the lady censor that I could replace it by 'tits,' as that was what working people called it, she threw me out of her office." His taste for the vernacular continues to offend people with ideological allegiances. Angela Carter, who seemed anxious to maintain her credentials as a Correct Thinker when she reviewed *The Miracle Game* for the *New York Times Book Review*, took huge offense because one of the characters, Dr. Gellen, "is described at one point as a woman chaser in vulgar anatomical language that is enough to put you off him for life."[7] She puts the blame on the translator, Paul Wilson, but it is a safe bet that it should go on Skvorecky, whose English is, after all, good enough to permit him to teach American literature at the University of Toronto for twenty years. Anyway, it's not the four-letter word beginning with *c* that identifies the object of the randy doctor's chasing, it's the five-letter one beginning with *p*, the one that is used as an affectionate name for cats. She also took umbrage because the narrator-hero describes a girl sporting a heavy and impressively widespread suntan as "brown as a nigger," though she could scarcely expect a young Czech male in need of a hyperbole in the middle of the 1950s to describe the girl as "brown as an Afro-American."

There is a lot more to *The Miracle Game* than a few raucous expressions that might offend properly trained sensibilities. It is the first novel that Skvorecky wrote after he left Czechoslovakia in 1969, though an English translation wasn't published until 1990; I would describe it as both an explanation of why he had to leave and a demonstration of what freedom can do for a novelist who has been thirsting for it. As explanation it is completely convincing. Danny Smiricky (seemingly Skvorecky's alter ego) has tried diligently to accommodate himself to life in a communist state. Absolutely incapable of believing the nonsense the party peddles, he has worked at not believing in anything, and he is too devout a coward to indulge in even the slyest forms of opposition. He prides himself on the acuteness of his sense of fear, judging it the most important gift a man can have who wants to survive in a state like this. So, if they want him to go teach social science at a girls school in a small town after completing his military service, he goes and teaches, even though he knows nothing about social science and the ministry has neglected to supply him with a course description and a textbook. If later he can't publish the sorts of things he wants to write, he learns how to turn out innocuous musical comedies. When the so-called Prague Spring comes along he doesn't join the chorus of writers singing the praises of liberalization, nor does he join in the hopeless demonstrations when the Soviet tanks come

7. Josef Skvorecky, *Talkin' Moscow Blues*, 45–46; Angela Carter, "A Magical Moment in Prague," 36.

rumbling into Wenceslas Square. Yet he cannot suppress his sense of the ridiculous and he cannot stop himself from liking the people he likes. That means he cannot last much longer in Czechoslovakia. He must go into exile or he will die, certainly figuratively, quite possibly literally as well. People who are having trouble understanding why the communist governments of Eastern Europe collapsed as swiftly and as completely as they did as soon as their Soviet props were pulled from under them could get all the enlightenment they need from *The Miracle Game.*

But it would be a shame to read such an energetically artful novel as though it were a text for dim-witted CIA agents. To put it in terms of technique, it is a novel that jumps back and forth in time covering a period of about fifteen years in the life of Danny Smiricky; more unusually, it also switches back and forth, sometimes even within a single sentence, among three narrative modes: an idyllic mode for dealing with personal, especially sexual relationships, a satiric mode for dealing with societal matters, and an adaptation of a mystery story mode for dealing with matters of religion. To put it in terms of theme, it celebrates human foolishness and decency, it damns ideology, and it puzzles over religion as being both a con game and a deeply satisfying affirmation of mystery. If that sounds complicated, it is; yet the novel as a whole is entirely unpretentious. It never gives an inch to that urge to impress that makes so many so-called postmodern novels a distinct pain to read. Skvorecky so carefully dramatizes a wide streak of dopiness in Danny—and by inevitable extension, in himself—that solemn, gullible people are misled into thinking that the complexities are all accidental and complain that he slips into telling funny stories when he ought to be sticking to serious social criticism.

One thing leads to another, one mode slides into another all through *The Miracle Game.* Traditional but still funny farce about the older girls in the school trying to seduce Danny when he cannot possibly give in to seduction because he has a painful venereal infection slides into the scene where a statue of St. Joseph seems to have made a gesture of benediction during a priest's sermon, and that in turn becomes the center of a mystery story that will not yield a definite solution, though the priest was most definitely beaten to death by the secret police as they were attempting to persuade him to recant his faith. The account of the efforts of the warmhearted woman who is the principal of the school to get all of her girls graduated, even the ones from politically suspect families, produces another scene of classic farce when the examiners from the Ministry of Education are stuffed with food, wine, and tranquilizers so that they will forget all about the examination; but that fades into the moment that comes years later, during the Prague Spring, when that same woman, having been falsely denounced as a tool of the party in the now-liberal newspapers, locks the door to her office and hangs herself with a piece of clothesline. Or to reverse the emphasis, a nightmarish scene at the Writer's Union in 1968 exposing the terrible intellectual contortions some writers put themselves through in order to stay in favor with the party is periodically interrupted with low comedy scenes of a hack trying to get up his courage to sign a petition that practically everybody else in the union has already signed. Nothing stays simple. Nothing stays funny. But nothing stays unfunny, either. One thing qualifies another, always. It's quite a game.

The history of our miserable century is full of stories of artists and writers being driven into exile by political stupidity and viciousness, but I am not sure any responded to that painful fate more exuberantly than Skvorecky did. Judging by what has subsequently been translated into English, he was a highly accomplished novelist while he was still living in Czechoslovakia coping with the demands of a sleazy system of state censorship. *The Cowards* is a powerful and influential first novel. *The Republic of Whores*, which I prefer to think of as *The Tank Corps*, a literal translation of its original Czech title, is a raucous, funny, devastating account of life among the unwilling members of the Czech army in the early fifties. "The Bass Saxophone" is one of those rarities that novelists dream about as they pile rough draft on top of rough draft, a beautifully condensed, evocative novella that poured out of his typewriter in three ecstatic days. *The Mournful Demeanor of Lieutenant Boruvka* earned a large audience for the way it combined something of English stories of deduction with something of European *romans policiers* to form an oblique kind of social criticism. And *Miss Silver's Past*, the last novel he wrote in Czechoslovakia, is a half-farce, half-mystery that is wholly worth rereading. Nonetheless, *The Miracle Game* is notches better than any of them, and it launched Skvorecky into a period of astonishing productivity.

In 1983 an interviewer for *Canadian Fiction Magazine* asked Skvorecky if he felt at home in Canada. "I feel very much at home in Canada," he replied. "I don't even like to travel to Europe as Canadians do, because I have become so attached to this country, to the atmosphere it has. Because—this is probably hard to explain—in my life, since I was fourteen, I have never experienced this atmosphere of liberal freedom. I have always lived under some kind of dictatorship where you had to turn around if you had to say something aloud. If you wrote anything, you had to think twice before you formulated a sentence, because you knew this would be tough for the censors. The secret police were always after you, and you were taken in for interrogation because of some stupid thing. So I value the atmosphere of liberal freedom that most people here don't realize they have, because for them it's like the air."[8]

In 1973 he completed one linked collection of detective stories, *Sins for Father Knox,* and another in 1975, *The End of Lieutenant Boruvka,* sandwiching between them in 1974 a memoir that had to sit in his drawer until 1996, when it was published under the title *Headed for the Blues.* In 1975 he also completed six stories about Danny Smiricky that come together to form something like a novel, *The Swell Season.* Two years later came *The Engineer of Human Souls,* a long, intricate novel that deals with all of the stages of Danny Smiricky's voyage from his small town in Czechoslovakia to a niche on the faculty of "Edenvale College" in Toronto. That was followed in 1981 by *The Return of Lieutenant Boruvka,* a fond kidding of the Czech community in Toronto in the guise of a mystery story. In 1983 he turned toward history with *Dvorak in Love,* a fiction grounded in fact that centers on Anton Dvorak's involvement with America and American music in the 1890s. *Talkin' Moscow Blues,* a collection of interviews and articles, most of which he wrote in English after coming to Toronto, was published in 1988. In 1992 he published a long historical novel about a group of Czechs who fought in the Civil War in Sherman's army that was not translated until 1996, and in 1997 he published, in English, *The Tenor Saxophonist's Story,* which is, like *The Swell Season,* a collection of stories that come to-

8. Skvorecky, *Talkin',* 341–42.

gether to form a novel. Through most of those years he also taught American literature in the University of Toronto and helped his wife run Sixty-Eight Publishers, a house devoted to the works Czech writers could not publish in their homeland. The publishing house has now gone happily out of business, but Skvorecky has no plans for leaving Canada, where the air has been so very good for him.

The Miracle Game can be seen as Skvorecky's first response to release from the constraints of state censorship. He can now give free rein to his gift for classic farce; his criticism of the party becomes bleaker and harsher; and for the first time he can acknowledge the pull of Czech Catholicism on his mind and imagination. *The Swell Season*, then, can be seen as his first full response to the experience of being free, much fuller and much more intense than he expressed in the detective stories he was writing in these years. Political and ideological concerns nearly disappear from the world of the novel and it becomes what the subtitle proclaims it to be, "A text on the most important things in life." The most important things in Danny Smiricky's young life are, sensibly enough, playing jazz and chasing girls, especially chasing girls. Canadian and American critics being on the whole a solemn lot, many would join the interviewer for *Canadian Fiction Magazine* in wondering if *The Swell Season* can really be an important book for Skvorecky, it's so cheerful, so celebratory, so free of either pride or guilt. It is. It's important to Skvorecky because it is faithful to the truth of his experience: "This is about a young boy who is after the girls. He cannot get any, but he never gives up, and he's happy and unhappy. And from time to time from the background comes this danger because I couldn't ignore it: the war. But this is how we lived."[9] It's a book that ought to be important to American readers, too, because it does not fit any of our preconceptions about novels of adolescence and might, therefore, force or charm us into taking a second look at our notions about both novels and adolescence. It is not a coming-of-age novel, replete with rites of initiation; nor is it a novel about threatened and/or triumphant innocence. Nor is it a more or less steamy account of sexual exploits and gifts, for the hero never catches any of the girls he chases. It is simply a bemused, amused, undisturbed

9. Ibid., 350.

account of boys and girls chasing and being chased around the mulberry bush. Boys expect to chase and girls to be chased. Sooner or later the chasing will end and they will all get on with the business of being adults; meanwhile, they enjoy being who they are and doing what they do. A vision of adolescent sexuality so free of Puritanism of either the old-fashioned religious variety or the up-to-date social scientific sort is refreshing; a novel that embodies that vision in an aesthetically sound way is indeed important.

Throughout the Danny Smiricky series, as in all sane comedy, self-pity is the occasion for laughter rather than tears. In *The Swell Season* Danny tries to feel sorry for himself because God won't keep the various bargains Danny has struck with him and because practically everybody in town is gleefully keeping track of the number of girls he has failed to talk into his arms—twenty-two, twenty-three if you allow for the fact that "one" of them was a pair of identical twins playing tricks on him. But he is finally too fond of all of the people he is sharing his season with to keep feeling sorry for himself. In *The Engineer of Human Souls,* the last novel in the series, Skvorecky has to deal with the comic artist's most painful truth, that many of the people he has loved have suffered pitiful fates while he himself has passed from one piece of good luck to another. He has to grieve for them and rejoice for himself, but he absolutely must keep those two emotions totally separated. Any smugness or any guilt will be grounds for excommunication from the muses.

He succeeds. And his necessary summing up from his safe haven in Toronto justifies not only its title but also its subtitle and even its six epigraphs. The title makes mocking reference to the definition of a writer attributed to Stalin: "as an engineer constructs a machine, so must a writer construct the mind of the New Man." The old-fashioned subtitle promises, with tongue only half in cheek, *An Entertainment on the Old Themes of Life, Women, Fate, Dreams, the Working Class, Secret Agents, Love and Death.* Of the six epigraphs I will quote only my own favorite: " 'To Generalize is to be an Idiot. To Particularize is the Alone Distinction of Merit. General Knowledges are those Knowledges that Idiots possess.'—William Blake." In short, *The Engineer of Human Souls* is a remarkably accomplished piece of work—downright gaudy, even, as Mark Twain might have said.

The Canadian critic George Woodcock thought that it was the most interesting novel published in Canada during the 1980s. He quotes with amusement from the interview in *Canadian Fiction Magazine* I cited earlier, observing that "Skvorecky presented himself in high camouflage as essentially an autobiographical novelist of a rather simple kind." Thus: "I just belong to those writers who base their writings on personal experience." And: "I simply described the events as they appeared to me, and as they appeared to most people." And best of all: "I am a simple realist. I try to capture my life experiences, and it so happened that I lived under dictatorships, so they are always in the background." Woodcock realizes that *The Engineer*—and by extension, the others in the Danny Smiricky series—are essentially novels about history. That is, they are novels in which "the effects of political events and systems shape the lives of the characters. [Their] moving impetus lies in the interaction between the domineering state and the individual who sets out to resist or evade it."[10] I would add that also they are not nearly so autobiographical as they seem to be. Danny Smiricky may share many of the public facts, so to speak, of Skvorecky's life, but he is always—even in *The Cowards*—a carefully drawn character, a piece of the mirror that Skvorecky has artfully set in the roadway to reflect the reality of his and our times, and as things turned out, the reality of his own transformation from a Czech and a European into a Canadian and an American.

His account of his long, stubborn resistance to the capital-H History that totalitarians celebrate having come to its comically triumphant conclusion, Skvorecky could turn to the study of the uncapitalized history that free men acknowledge, to the past that can illuminate the present. Perhaps I should state that more bluntly. The theorists of totalitarianism argue for a deterministic view of history and see it culminating in the state, which rightly commands the absolute loyalty of individuals; Skvorecky's multivolume account of Danny Smiricky's life demonstrates how thoroughly wrong their argument is. With that job done, he could pay tribute to the history that free men and women have known and made and

10. George Woodcock, "The Unforgivable Sin of Ignorance: Notes on *The Engineer of Human Souls*," 143–44.

that he can now rightly claim as his. He first does so obliquely and lyrically in *Dvorak in Love: A Light-Hearted Dream* and then directly and exuberantly in *The Bride of Texas.*

I wish there were an established term for describing the role that Dvorak plays for Skvorecky. Dvorak can't be called his alter ego—for a Czech that would be something close to blasphemy—but Dvorak is the means for his re-creating and thereby capturing the lighthearted history that the totalitarians sought to deny to him and to everyone else. That's foggy, but the idea is essentially simple. Truthfulness to the facts of Dvorak's life and music, especially to his two stays in America in the mid-1890s and to the remarkable use he made of the music of black Americans of the period, requires Skvorecky to explore the historical roots of major aspects of his own life, especially his love of jazz and of American life in general, and the effort to imagine Dvorak as a character in his novel puts him into a peculiarly intimate relationship with those historical roots. Between them, the historical Dvorak and the fictional Dvorak give to Skvorecky an amorous, jazzy, half-American, half-Czech past that has nothing to do with any ideology and a great deal to do with a delight in freedom. The novel is what it claims to be, *A Light-Hearted Dream,* but it is also, necessarily, an exceedingly sophisticated work of art. Owlish critics who think that anything lighthearted must be simple and therefore easy should plot the time line of the narrative and—for good measure—summarize Skvorecky's account of the processes of musical composition.

Dvorak in Love is in so many ways such an intimate exploration of aesthetic and psychological issues that a reader can easily forget it is a historical novel based on a great deal of skillful research; not so *The Bride of Texas,* which has the heft (609 pages) and subject matter (the Civil War), though not the heaving bosoms and empty heads, of a conventional best-seller. Actually, *The Bride* is driven by the same deeply personal need to find a usable past and it carries only one bold step further the techniques for blending fact and fiction that he developed in *Dvorak,* that indeed he had been working on throughout the Danny Smiricky series. In the Smiricky stories that blending is not a noticeable problem because the reader knows nothing about the actual persons. In *Dvorak* it's a somewhat delicate problem because any reader, even one who is not a Czech, is practically certain to know something about Antonin Dvorak and his music, and perhaps a little about the black musicians who figure as secondary characters in the novel; it's hard to do justice to both the actual and the fictional characters. In *The Bride of Texas* the problem is extremely difficult, for he has to give fictional freshness and fluidity to characters and events most of us have studied and argued about in and out of history courses. That he succeeds is a tribute in part to his technical sophistication and in part to his need to forge links for himself and his fellow refugees from the communist world with the past of the world they have become part of.

Near the end of his essay on *The Engineer of Human Souls,* in the course of arguing that Skvorecky has a true affinity with the Canadian-born writer Margaret Laurence, George Woodcock speaks of "the ultimately nationless world of literature."[11] Skvorecky and his characters, whether entirely fictional or not, are citizens of a nationless world as we all are when we immerse ourselves in literature. I will gladly argue my own American-born affinity with him and his characters, no matter how badly I mispronounce their names. In the very useful phrase of Hemingway's Count Mippipopolous he is "one of us." I would point out to the literary purists that the more freely I read good novels in translation the more capacious and the more interesting that pronoun *us* becomes.

Postscript

Having been corresponding with Josef Skvorecky for the past two or three years, I sent him a copy of this chapter when it was nearly finished, mainly so that he could correct any mistakes of fact that I might have made about his work, but also so that he could see what I was saying about the whole matter of translation, for we had frequently touched on it in our letters. Josef (that's the letter writer; the novelist remains "Skvorecky") is a generous man and heaped praise on the quality of my understanding of his work. My point, and Josef's, too, is that though I was totally reliant on translations I could come to an understanding at least equal to that reached by critics who could read it in the original Czech. That puts quite a dent

11. Ibid., 150.

in Professor McCormick's purist argument: Skvorecky himself testifies that I was reading Skvorecky, not merely Paul Wilson or Kaca
Polackova Henley or any of his other hardworking translators.

Josef went on to offer some most interesting comments on the
matter of reading work in translation:

"You are of course absolutely right about the silliness of the su-
perpurist stance which demands that people read books only in the
original languages, and if they are too lazy to master the thirty or so
languages of the most advanced cultures, they should stay at home
in the sense of restricting their reading to the lingo they grew up in.
Anyway, this impossible perfectionism is so typical of someone
who was born into a major language with a rich literature so that to
read in other languages is not such an absolute necessity as with
people born into "small" languages. If I knew only Czech—which,
unfortunately, is the case of some literary critics in Prague—I doubt
I would ever have been able to become a fiction writer. . . . I grew
up on translations of American (and to some extent British) books
in translations that were often far from good, and yet, somehow, the
world of the original, the spirit of the writer, whatever it was, came
through. Even that awful first Czech translation of *A Farewell to
Arms*, where the translator never realized that lovers who speak
Czech go at some point from the polite 'you' to the intimate
'thou'—even that absolute translatorial blunder I read with interest.
It is true—but then this is an extreme case of an extremely bad
translation—that I realized what a thing of beauty Hemingway's dialogue was only when I read it in English, shortly after the war in a
Swedish edition. But I fell in love with Poe when I was about nine
and reading that translation now, with all my translator's and
writer's experience, I can see what a poor job it was. And yet, Poe
remained in my heart, even with all of the crudities of the translation added to his—in contemporary American opinion—unwieldy
prose.

"And . . . some classics can even be 'improved' by translation,
I.e. by rendering their text into a more lively, more contemporary
idiom. After World War II, *The Canterbury Tales* was a big best-seller
thanks to Frantisek Vrba's translation, and so were many American
and English classics whom my students [in Toronto] usually found
too difficult to read due to their nineteenth century diction.

"The poetry: in Czech, there is a long tradition of translating rhymed poetry in rhymes, and some translators achieved a real mastery. Vitezslav Nezval, the great Czech surrealist poet, a natural-born rhyming genius has done many of the best poems by Poe so beautifully, that they are probably more effective to contemporary Czech readers than Poe's originals are to contemporary Americans (and as Baudelaire's translations are said to have been for his French readers.)"[12]

12. Josef Skvorecky, letter to the author, November 24, 1996.

6

Thinking Uncertainly

Language, as Walker Percy had the good sense to stress, is talk, a collaborative enterprise between two people who are endeavoring to reach a shared understanding of the relationship between a symbol (a word) and the concept it refers to. *Endeavoring* is the key word here: it may take more than one or two tries, and they may or may not manage to reach reasonably full agreement, though if the matter they are talking about is very complex, either intellectually or emotionally, some degree of misunderstanding is likely to persist. That fuzziness, that lack of sharp-edged understanding, vexes people who pride themselves on the clarity of their minds and yearn for logic and order in their lives rather than variety and vitality, but that's the quality that makes language go. Outrageous as it may seem to ideologues, a generous amount of uncertainty is the essential lubricant for human communication. If the same word couldn't carry different meanings under different circumstances and in different contexts, if many words didn't possess emotional connotations as well as intellectual denotations, if we didn't have to keep finding different ways of saying much the same thing, conversation would lose all its savor and social life would wither. If words were in a simple, firm, one-to-one relationship with the concepts and things they refer to, the simplest books would be too heavy to carry in a wheelbarrow. Derrida, Barthes, de Man, and the other prophets of deconstruction in the seventies and eighties who were offended by the ambiguity of languages were the intellectual kin of scientists of the twenties and thirties who couldn't accept Heisenberg's demonstration of uncertainty lurking at the heart of matter. Both groups, it must be said, are in the position of children stamping their feet and crying, "But reality *ought* to be clear and reasonable."

Perhaps I am cheating a trifle by using quantum physics' term *uncertainty* in a discussion of linguistic and literary matters. In physics it has precise significance, originating in the verifiable fact that an attempt to measure the velocity of a subatomic particle makes it impossible to measure its mass, and vice versa; here its meaning is anything but precise, referring to the observable truth that you can't be sure about all sorts of important things in language and literature. But I want to use the term as a metaphor in order to insist that just as you cannot make sense of the way reality works at the subatomic level until you accept the validity of Heisenberg's uncertainty principle, you cannot make valid sense about language and literature until you acknowledge that they are permeated by qualities whose effects and significance you cannot fully measure and express however strongly you respond to them.

Analysis is difficult enough with simple linguistic communications—with chitchat about the weather and TV programs, letters home, and thank-you notes. When we start trying to think about communications of the highest order of complexity and meaning, works of literature, the sources and the levels of uncertainty multiply until we need not one but several Heisenbergs to enunciate not one but a bundle of uncertainty principles. In some not necessarily extravagant moods I am willing to declare that everything about literature is full of uncertainty for everybody involved with it; but at the same time I would insist that the greater the work the more enriching and the more abundant the uncertainty is. Witness Shakespeare. Who but a fool would volunteer to give a short, clear explanation of *King Lear* or *As You Like It*, and who but a bubbleheaded reviewer out to win a reputation for sauciness would deny the greatness of those works? Bring everything you have to bear on repeated encounters with great works of literature and you still won't reach bottom in them; they remain fresh and mysterious, a little deeper than you can dive. But that's all right; they remain that way for the writers who wrote them, too. If Shakespeare could have explained the last act of *The Tempest* or Cervantes part 2 of *Don Quixote*, they wouldn't have had to write them.

It's nice to say such things. They give a release to the emotions of gratitude and joy that one feels in the presence of art, but they do very little for the understanding that a critic is obliged to serve. To get a useful handle on some of the uncertainties we need to understand, I would observe that the literary work, which embodies and exploits major uncertainties of its own, stands between two notable uncertainties, a writer and a reader, both of whom have something like multiple personalities and neither of whom is fully aware of what he or she is doing.

Take the writer first. The actual human being, the social being who lives as other social beings do and gladly accepts all royalty checks, is responsible for what gets written but turns the work of writing over to another, quite different self. That second self, who may or may not bear any great resemblance to the actual human being, is the person that the reader senses behind the work and is often for many readers the deepest, most compellingly attractive force in the work. Biographers like to assume that the two are so nearly alike that all their scrounging in records and letters and reminiscences of friends will illuminate the work, but they are kidding themselves. The actual P. G. Wodehouse, for example, was a very nice, gentle man, a faithful husband who was kind to animals and pleasant to nearly everyone, and all-in-all as dull a fellow as you are ever likely to come across; the Wodehouse you meet in those great farcical stories was a man who could keep you giggling with delight year after year after year. "Plum," as the actual man was called by those close to him, never missed an installment of his favorite soap opera; Wodehouse was the great master in twentieth-century fiction of comic figures of speech (e.g., Bertie Wooster speaking of times of crisis in his family "when Aunt is calling to Aunt like mastodons bellowing across primeval swamps").[1] The author of *The Code of the Woosters* may be an extravagant case, but it is plain, simple, and commonplace truth that the actual person is seldom the charismatic equal of the person one has come to know intimately in reading a good novel. Charming people, I think, seldom write good novels, probably because charming people can't bring themselves to expend their finest qualities on getting a story told.

Matters get even more complicated when the self behind the novel tells a first-person narrative, particularly when the narrator is a major character in the story bearing little or no resemblance to the self. Take, for a gorgeous example, the virtuoso performance in

1. P. G. Wodehouse, *The World of Jeeves*, 241.

Adventures of Huckleberry Finn, where the reader is always aware of the difference between Huck doing the narrating and Twain managing the novel, and seldom aware of the very great difference between Mark Twain and Samuel Clemens. And that's putting it too simply. When Samuel Clemens settled down to being Mark Twain he could give a chameleon lessons in changing apparent selves. If all of that does not create enough uncertainty, consider the extent to which characters in a novel are projections of the novelist's personality and experience. How could, say, a Henry James move so convincingly into the interiors of so many major characters in so many different novels if they were not all, no matter what their gender, aspects of his own self? Or if James is not your cup of tea, take *War and Peace* and explain which of the dozen or so major characters in that novel do and which do not show you something about the nature of Count Leo Tolstoy? If the novel is the most highly autobiographical of forms, it is also the most deceptive, most elusive form of autobiography.

The reader is a greater, possibly much greater, source of uncertainty than the writer. At least the writer is a person with highly developed gifts for communication who is concentrating very hard on the double-edged task of knowing what needs to be said and saying it so that a reader has a decent chance of understanding it; the actual reader can be this, that, or the other, with varying capacities for concentration and imagination, and with a dismaying variety of possible purposes. That's just the actual reader, the one with a name and address. That uncertain citizen has to play a role, act the part of a reader of the given work; what is more, he or she had better have the ability and the willingness to make that part similar to the part of the ideal reader that the work implicitly defines, or failing that, have the wit to be thoroughly aware of the differences between the two versions and make appropriate allowances for them. People who cannot delight in role-playing—who have nothing of the ham actor in them—cannot be good students and critics of literature; on the other hand, no one can play all the different kinds of parts that different literary works demand of their readers. If a work asks you to pretend to be a kind of person you either cannot stand to be or do not know how to be, you cannot do an adequate job of reading it. Just as even the best actors encounter parts beyond their reach, the

best critics encounter books they cannot respond to appropriately—
of course, experienced critics, like experienced actors, know how to
fake an adequate response.

There is no sense in deploring the uncertainties in language that
are the lubricant making conversation and communication possible, nor is there any sense in deploring the treacheries of role-
playing that permeate the writing and the reading of literature. A
sensible writer admits to himself that he does not fully understand
what he is doing; rather than trying to push the work around,
rather than getting bossy with it, he turns the major decisions over
to a part of the mind over which he has relatively little conscious
control and which is plainly, even notoriously, content with irra-
tionalities. Or if you'd prefer a way of putting it that avoids the pit-
falls of psychological explanation, a sensible writer trusts that story
that the fates have given him and devotes whatever energy, skill,
and intelligence he possesses to doing what it requires him to do.
Similarly, a good reader doesn't waste time and energy demanding
that the work come to him on his own terms; first, he submits to it
so that he can get the reading done and then later he will use all of
the intellect he has (and probably wish for more) in an effort to explain to himself and others what came from that reading. The uncertainties of literature are destructive only to those who would, out
of either pride or ignorance, deny them; those who submit to them
quickly realize that they open up to an experience that makes ordinary discourse seem paltry.

Thank God for the written word—that is, for the text. We might
want to argue almost endlessly about the interpretation of the
work, but once the text has been established (I will skip over the
possible difficulties of getting one established), that collection of
words and punctuation marks is a matter of fact, the one unchang-
ing presence in the midst of compounding uncertainties. That
makes it the rock to which all sensible critics, like all sensible writers, cling in the same way and for the same reason that Thoreau
clung to such facts as the bubbles in the ice as he sought to comprehend the constantly changing appearance of Walden Pond. Any
truth is indeed better than make-believe. For a comic illustration of
a writer and a critic clinging to that rock, which will also cast light
on some other matters, I can cite a few letters that passed between

me and another literary pen pal of mine, George V. Higgins, in May and June of 1995.

George (once again, that's the letter writer; the novelist remains Higgins) had lent me a couple of weeks earlier his video copy of the uncut, unreleased version of the movie they made from his first novel, *The Friends of Eddie Coyle,* an engrossing, thoroughly unsentimental account of a small-time crook in Boston who gets tangled up with some hard guys and winds up dead. By sheer good luck, the cleaned up, somewhat cut, and somewhat sanitized version that was released to the theaters showed up on the American Movie Channel while what I now think of as the "original" version was still fresh enough in mind that I could be specific about differences between the two.

I wrote George the next day (May 27, 1995), noting first the damage that had been done to the movie when they tamed the profanity in the dialogue for the released version and then the still greater damage done when they made what must have seemed like some minor changes in the story that the novel told. "That cleaned up dialogue," I said, "just doesn't ring true. I am more convinced than ever that the role of dialogue in movies is greatly underrated." (I was picking up on an exchange in earlier letters about what he had been told by Paul Monash, who wrote the script for the movie, to the effect that movies don't need and can't use lengthy speeches of the sort that his novels luxuriate in, what characters say in a movie being far less important than what the camera shows them doing.) In a novel or in a movie, I argued, if you don't get the talk right the characters don't exist, and nobody this side of a postmodern theorist wants to read a book or see a movie about characters that don't exist. "In short, they blew a hole in a good scene when they wouldn't let the hippie girl who was buying the machine guns persuade the seller of the seriousness of their purposes by saying that they wanted them to rob a *fucking* bank." Then I drifted into a criticism of both versions: "And they blew a sizable hole in the whole story when they wouldn't let Scalisi [the leader of the bank-robbing crew] tell Eddie about how fast his 'stew' [the stewardess named Wanda he was living with] would come when he stuck his hand down her crotch." I admitted that in the seventies when the movie was made, they couldn't possibly have kept that line in, even though it's as quick a way as you could hope to find of characterizing the raw masculine crudity of someone like Scalisi, "but couldn't they have managed some way of keeping in the business of her tipping off the cops to the coming robbery because Scalisi had outraged her by telling Eddie about her sexual urgencies? I do think we were supposed to notice that lots of people have lots of reasons for dropping a dime on bad guys in the bank robbery business; that's why it's such a risky business. Also, neither Eddie, who was killed because he was thought to have done it, nor Dillon, who the movie suggests did it, knew enough to set up Scalisi's crowd that way." My general point was that the moviemakers failed to notice how very tightly woven the novel's story is. I finished by complaining that when the director changed the details of Dillon's killing of Eddie in order to get the flashy visual effect of the bullet hole opening up in the side window of the car, he lost the oppressive sense of Dillon's careful work as an executioner—"six slugs from a .22, all of which will stay inside the skull, are guaranteed to destroy any brain."

George takes accuracy every bit as seriously as I do. "I have to offer some correction to your *Coyle* exegesis," he wrote on June 5, 1995. "Wanda didn't dump Scalisi and his pals because he bragged about how readily he could light her off. She dumped him because he hit her. Dillon didn't shoot Coyle six times with the Arminius centerfire .22; he shot him twice. You're quite right about the slug exiting the skull; it would not have. I know this because I unsuccessfully prosecuted [when he was an Assistant Federal Attorney] the case of a guy who got two behind the left ear from an Arminius centerfire .22 and the bullets didn't come out."

I returned to the discussion (June 11, 1995) crowing that "I am not the only guy whose memory of the text of *Eddie Coyle* is not to be trusted." I admitted that I had forgotten that Scalisi had slapped her across the face but argued that her fury over his gossiping about her sexuality with Coyle is much more emphatically dealt with. In point of fact, I had informed myself by rereading, no indication of her motive is given when she tips off her friend from the state police. "Maybe the author thought to himself that it was the slapping that did it, but he neglected to state that in the text. Still, if I had been careful I would have mentioned the slapping as well as the gossiping."

Crowing on, I claimed that I was closer to being right about the killing than George was. He specified two shots, apparently because it was two in the real case that prompted the fictional one; I specified six shots because I was sure Dillon had fired until he hit empty and not knowing beans about a "twenty-two magnum Arminius revolver" (or any other kind of revolver) I assumed that like the guns in the Westerns it held six shots. My rereading showed that Dillon, who was sitting in the backseat, did fire the whole load into the back of dead-drunk Eddie's head, and when the kid, who had started driving the car much too fast, explained that he got nervous because there were "so many" shots, Dillon said "there was nine of them." God knows where I got the information that .22 slugs do not go all the way through the skull—probably from accounts of the assassination of Robert Kennedy.

George's next letter (June 20, 1995) called a truce. "Of course I returned at once to *Eddie Coyle,* and there ascertained that indeed Dillon did empty the Arminius *centerfire* .22 into Eddie's head. All nine shots. To be completely candid, as Richard Nixon used to say, I dunno whether a centerfire, much more powerful than a rimfire, might not have penetrated the head and crazed the car window. Twenty-four years later, I don't think I'll worry about it—the Statute's tolled."

I can believe that anyone coming across those letters and reading them in sequence would think the pair of us were putting on a ridiculous performance quibbling at length over trivial matters; but actually we were enacting fundamental responsibilities of critics and novelists. As George has observed in other letters, as well as in the textbook he wrote for his students, *On Writing: Advice for Those Who Write to Publish (or Would Like To),* "the writer is always at the mercy of his story."[2] That means that some stories are better than other stories and that explains, he tells his students, why steady improvement is a rarity in the career of writers. Writers, like all other artists, are not bound to and cannot be judged by any rule of progress, for they have to work with the stories that come to them as gifts, and can't afford to be too picky about what ones they will accept. But they are bound to do their best by any story they write; they cannot, as I said earlier, play fast and loose with it, they must

2. Higgins, *On Writing,* 85.

pay the most careful attention they can manage to even its most trivial-seeming details. The great modern architect Mies van der Rohe might have been overstating it when he said that "God is in the details," but unquestionably the devil lies in wait for architects and writers—not to mention critics—who blur the details.

Higgins was doing the proper work of a serious novelist when he realized that Scalisi would assault the stewardess both physically and psychically and that Wanda would strike back by giving the cops all the information they needed to trap Scalisi and his friends on their next scheduled bank robbery; he was making his story and its characters thicker, more densely established. I was doing the proper work of a serious critic when I got those details of the story clear in my mind; Scalisi became more forcefully, though quite unconsciously, a man bent on destroying himself and Wanda became a more complex, morally challenging character, much more interesting than a stereotypical "stew." Similarly, when I got entirely clear on the facts of Dillon's execution of Eddie I got a clearer, more horrifying understanding of a stone-cold killer's mind and of the disproportions of Eddie's fate. (True, he was a small-time crook, and true, he had decided to betray his old friend Scalisi to the Feds in order to get a lighter sentence for his own involvement in the hijacking of a truckload of cigarettes, though he waited a little too long to do it to get credit for cooperating with the authorities. But nine slugs in his head?) The director of the movie version of *Eddie Coyle* did a lot of good work, but lacking Higgins's principled dedication to the story and his disciplined concern for the facts of the fiction, he settled a little too easily for flashy effects and conventional characterizations. If he had pushed a little harder he could have come up with a brilliant, memorable movie instead of a merely pretty good one; but of course he had the whole weight of the Hollywood system pushing against him.

I think that in taking the positions we do with respect to the primacy of the story and of what I term the facts of the fiction Higgins and I are responding effectively to the essential—that is, the fundamental and necessary—uncertainties of literature. No childish footstamping for us. He does it by putting into command of the work, so to speak, a nonrational force—a sense of story rather than a sense of meaning. A sense of meaning calls for logic and argument; in defiance of the essential uncertainties, it strives for clarity and certainties. Stories, on the other hand, are not supposed to yield certainties; they don't come to sound conclusions, only to possible meanings and satisfying endings. I respond to the essential uncertainties by embracing stories, by distrusting my intellectual fondness for categories and interpretations, and by insisting that I read accurately before I indulge in brilliance of any sort.

But that is a highly abstract explanation to which I shall return later; for now, a less fancy, more traditional one would be helpful. Higgins belongs squarely in the great tradition of American realism; among the writers he strongly recommends to his students in *On Writing* are Ring Lardner, James Thurber, Hemingway, John P. Marquand, Irwin Shaw, John O'Hara, Gay Talese, and William Manchester. Here and elsewhere he is particularly forceful in his admiration for the short stores of John O'Hara; like O'Hara, he would like to be able to claim that he "has recorded the history of his times and got it right." That tradition with its drive to "get it right" derives primarily from Mark Twain and *Huckleberry Finn,* as Hemingway argued in *Green Hills of Africa,* but it is also greatly influenced by Henry James, who articulated the necessity for granting the writer his *donnée,* which I would roughly define as the story that has been given to him to tell, and whose urgent advice to all writers was *specify, specify, specify.* One thing that Higgins and all of the writers he admires know is that those who *specify* do not have to stoop to explaining; also, in common with all creative people in all of the arts and sciences, they do not know where their central ideas came from. The creative act does not yield to the explications of the analytical mind.

I share Higgins's delight in the works of American realism and a very great deal of my understanding of what literary criticism should do is derived, both directly and indirectly, from Henry James. T. S. Eliot's oft-quoted comment that James "had a mind too fine to be violated by an idea" has always struck me as being more irritating than enlightening, but it's true that James knew quite exactly the place of the intellect in art and in life. I observe that his brother William had one of the finest intellects of his time, but William never did quite understand Henry's novels. As I suggested earlier, Milan Kundera probably had in mind something like this submission to the needs of the story when he spoke of true novelists listening for the suprapersonal wisdom of the novel; at least this gives us a way of understanding his claim that "great novels are always a little more intelligent than their authors." Exactly the same is true for the critic, who discovers the suprapersonal wisdom of the novel by submitting to the text; great novels are more intelligent than their critics, too.

The Friends of Eddie Coyle marks the beginning of Higgins's efforts to get it right about a substantial chunk of the history of his times. (Well, not quite the beginning; *fourteen* unpublished novels preceded it, but he consigned them to the dump the weekend after *Eddie* was accepted for publication.) Unfortunately, it also marks the beginning of a lamentable mislabeling of his work. It has so much about crime and criminals in it that whoever issued the shelving instructions for retailers jumped to the conclusion that it belonged in the crime/mystery section, some distance east of Agatha Christie's genteel mystifications and just west of Jack Higgins's hairy-chested money-makers. Once a conclusion like that gets jumped to in the book trade it stays jumped to: all of the twenty-odd novels and books that have followed have been ticketed for the same shelf.

Eddie Coyle simply is not a crime story or a piece of genre fiction of any kind; rather, it is a novel about people who commit crimes and like any good novel it shows you what their lives are like so that you may respond to them as you will. With one exception, none of Higgins's books are crime stories, and some of them scarcely touch on criminal activities. The one exception is *The Mandeville Talent*. It is specifically, according to the dust jacket, "a crime novel"; but though it attempts to be a nice, ordinary piece of genre fiction about the solution of a murder twenty years after it happened, it just plain doesn't work. Higgins is cocky enough and irascible enough to try a stunt like that because he was so sick and tired of having his novels mislabeled and, worse, missold as crime stories, but his mind is too lively, too impertinent to accept gracefully the constraints of that highly artificial form. It's a solidly professional piece of writing, of course, but I don't think that it came close to winning an "Edgar" from the Mystery Writers of America.

I feel sorry for the poor customer who grabs *A Choice of Enemies* off the shelf at his bookstore thinking it's a nice gory crime story and discovers when he settles down with it that night that it's a sympathetic account of a rogue elephant of a man who is Speaker of the Massachusetts House—or the one who gets partway into

Wonderful Years, Wonderful Years and finds a painfully credible account of a woman sinking through paranoia to suicide instead of a happy little tale about a romp down primrose paths. The four novels Higgins has published about his criminal lawyer, Jerry Kennedy, have nothing in common with the innumerable installments of Earle Stanley Gardner's Perry Mason series and very little with John Grisham's best-sellers about lawyers. But even the five relatively early novels that center on cops or criminals—*The Digger's Game, Cogan's Trade, The Judgment of Deke Hunter, The Rat on Fire,* and *The Patriot Game*—are not conventional crime stories. They take relatively little interest in suspense and excitement, nor do they celebrate the power and romance of gangsters in the fashion of the *Godfather* movies and their even more trashy clones. They are social histories of life among the pros and semipros of our criminal classes—genuine thieves, not frustrated lovers and desperate junkies.

The Digger's Game, published a year after *Eddie Coyle,* nicely illustrates where Higgins's interest lies. The central character, Digger Doherty, owns a flourishing workingman's bar, is happily married, and has a brother, Paul, who is a priest well on his way to becoming a bishop. But The Digger likes the criminal life and takes pride in his reputation as a hard case. He is also, in the immemorial fashion of self-confident members of successful classes, whether criminal or professional, sucker enough to sign up for a packaged tour to Las Vegas, get drunk playing at the blackjack table, and wind up owing the wise guys running the tour eighteen thousand dollars, which of course he doesn't have and can't get honestly. Yet a couple of small burglaries, a nice, cushy "robbery" of a furrier who wants to collect from his insurance company, and the "loan" of a few thousand from his brother get Digger off the hook soon enough. The novel ends with him in bed with his wife happily anticipating some solid domestic sex. The ending isn't quite so happy for others: Paul has scraped the bottom of his own barrel to get money for Digger; a friend of Digger's, who was planning to betray him to the FBI for the reward money, is about to be found dead; and the wise guys who were making money hand over fist running the tours have had a falling out, the cheapskate who thought he could save money by serving as his own hit man getting shot to death by the small-time loan shark, who was too stupid to understand what he had to do to make the scheme work well. The big scenes in the book—the ones that Higgins lays into with a relish—are not melodramatic: Digger's humiliating effort to get money from his brother, his nightmare in Las Vegas, and his reunion with old buddies as they go to pull off a robbery at the behest of its supposed victim. Higgins is interested in how a system for separating suckers from their money works or how experienced thieves go about looting a fur-storage, but he is so little concerned for melodramatic effects that the winner of the shoot-out quits the tour business in terror of getting in over his head again, and Digger's murder of the friend who was about to betray him is only hinted at. Compare *The Digger's Game* with any of the genre fictions that do belong in the Crime/Mystery section. The one follows a formula in ways that might be quite amusing to a compliant reader; the other goes where it has to go, though it does what it can to maintain the interest of an intelligent reader.

Yet the big, dazzling difference is in the language. Higgins, as I demonstrated earlier when I looked closely at those two chapters in *Sandra Nichols Found Dead,* has an astonishingly good ear for the ins and outs, ups and downs of American language. He can command for narrative purposes a plain style that flows like spring water, and he writes dialogue that is so good—so accurate and so subtly revealing—that for long stretches he can dispense almost entirely with narrative and let his characters speak for themselves. No genre writer can match him in this respect, not even Elmore Leonard, whose renditions of the speech of Detroit's criminals are much admired. In *The Digger's Game,* Higgins characterizes through their way of talking a successful priest, a hanger-on in a tough bar, a businessman gone crooked, a small-time loan shark, a wise guy who thinks he is a hard guy but isn't, and a wise guy who really is a hard guy, plus The Digger, who is a bartender that can be trusted not to cheat a widow, a faithful husband, a bad brother, and a very competent thief and killer, all rolled into one. If that range is not wide enough to impress you, go to *Dreamland,* a first-person narrative by a priggish lawyer from one of the tonier law firms in Boston who is, you gradually realize, mad as a hatter; or try the radical hippies and the rich women in *Outlaws,* or the newspaper publisher in *Impostors,* or the congressmen and assorted PR people in *A Year or So with Edgar* and *Victories.* Higgins can tune in on speech at all social levels in the cities and small towns of the East Coast, especially Boston and its environs.

For a nice, clear, simple illustration of his skill in rendering shades of usage in the vernacular, consider what he does with profanity. (Seeing such words in print has been known to paralyze the thought processes of some readers, but Higgins isn't trying to shock anybody, he is just trying to get things right. The truth is that when we are not guarding our speech many of us Americans are a tolerably foul-mouthed lot.) At one extreme you find Earl Beale in *Trust*, a used-car salesman who did time in a federal penitentiary for conspiring with gamblers to fix games when he was playing college basketball. Normally his speech is liberally sprinkled with profanity of all sorts, though he can clean it up when he's talking to a customer or his boss; when things go wrong, as they do when he stupidly tries to blackmail the wealthy businessman his girlfriend is frequently called upon to accompany for long weekends, Earl spins out of control. "You fucking bastard, you must think I'm fucking stupid. You give fucking Penny fifteen thousand fucking dollars for a fucking long weekend, and that's it, it's over with, like you just bought a dinner. And then you got the fucking nerve to tell me, knowing what I've got, and what I can do to you; you got the lousy fucking goddamned nerve to offer me just ten lousy fucking more? I could wreck your fucking life. I oughta blow your fucking car up. I could do that, you know. Fucking asshole big shot—who the fuck you think you are?"[3] That's not pretty, but it does come rushingly off an American tongue.

In *The Digger's Game*, he registers the difference between the nervous, small-time crook and the man connected with Mafiosi bosses by means of their profanity; the small-timer curses monotonously, compulsively, while the man who finally takes over the operation of the tours curses purposefully—just enough to show that he can be one of the boys, as long as nobody crosses him. Higgins does something more subtle in *The Rat on Fire*; first he catches the casual flow of the profanity when some state cops are talking among themselves and then lets you hear the false heaviness in their profanity when they are sitting at the counter in The Scandinavian Pastry Shop trying to pass themselves off as truck drivers.

Profanity is just another portion of the language and like all other portions it requires and rewards skill in its use. Higgins gives

3. Higgins, *Trust*, 185.

himself the pleasure of instructing students on this matter in *On Writing*. He reprints a short story of his called "A Small Matter of Consumer Protection"[4] that consists almost entirely of a dialogue between one Dennis Carnes, a lawyer who scratches out a living defending the drunk and disorderly types who supply most of the business for criminal court sessions, and Robert Shoate, a lawyer who makes a very good living defending mobsters. He then analyzes the dialogue carefully, showing how Carnes's false-hearty way of addressing Shoate reveals his envy, and how Shoate puts Carnes in his place with some fine-tuned responses. When Carnes implies that he has gone high-hat, Shoate pats him on the shoulder and unloads a few Irishisms on him. When Carnes turns aggressive by trying to shock him with an unexpected use of the word *fucking*, Shoate promptly gives a virtuoso performance with the word, first by using it in indirect quotations of his Italian client (whom Carnes despises, bigot-fashion) and then by using it just once himself.

Higgins has every right to boast of his skill and accuracy in writing dialogue, profane or otherwise. Certainly he pushes that skill as hard and as far as a novelist can, almost to the point of creating a new form, the operatic novel. Typically, a chapter in a Higgins novel consists of two or three characters talking to—sometimes at, rarely with—each other; when the wind is at his back and the moon over his left shoulder, a succession of chapters is like a succession of scenes in a lush opera, one aria after another with very little recitative for leavening. *The Rat on Fire* is a particularly clear and entirely successful example, though at a glance its story doesn't look like anything anyone would describe as operatic.

After a mere four sentences of preliminaries it breaks into aria: Detective Lieutenant John Roscommon of the Massachusetts State Police on the horrors of having to work with a prosecutor named Terry Mooney, "about thirty years old, got more hair on him 'n a fuckin' buffalo but less brains, and he's got this diploma from some half-assed law school and that gives him the right to order everybody around. He thinks. The little shit." Mooney, it develops, has just discovered that people are deliberately burning buildings down in Boston, and what is more, doing it for money. He has persuaded

4. Higgins, *On Writing*, 129–36.

the Attorney General to give him Roscommon and the two sergeants who work under him to nail the villains and thereby generate news stories about how good Mooney is and how smart it was of the AG, who is coming up for reelection, to appoint Mooney as a full-fledged prosecutor. "I have never had an ulcer," says (or sings) Roscommon. "I am fifty-eight years old and if I do say so myself, I am in the prime of health and the pink of fucking goddamned good condition. But if I ever get an ulcer, if I ever do fall down and collapse on the floor with motherfucking apoplexy, it will be the fault of Terry Mooney." However, being a smart and honest cop as well as a healthy one, Roscommon converts Mooney's impossible assignment to catch people setting fires into the very manageable, and personally satisfying, one of trapping a crooked fire marshal named Billy Malatesta and the loser who is bribing him, Leo Proctor.

Sooner or later each of the important characters gets to step forward and sing. Sometimes the arias last only a paragraph or two but a surprising number of them fill most of a chapter. Nearly all of the thirty other short chapters (the novel is only 183 pages long) are like the first one in combining highly energetic self-portraits with a surprising amount of storytelling. In summary, the story is sordid and dull: the owner of an apartment building in the slums hires an ex-convict to bribe a fire marshal and then burn his building, not knowing that the state police are conducting an undercover investigation; the building burns all right when the ex-con douses a bunch of rats with gasoline and sets them on fire as they run up the interior walls. Unfortunately, one tenant, a young black man named Alfred Davis, who stayed home from work one time too often, is still in the building at the time; when the fire escape collapses under his weight, their simple arson-for-profit becomes first-degree murder and the conspirators are easily persuaded to fink on each other. But fill in that summary a little, identify the apartment owner as a Jew, the apartment dwellers as blacks, the arsonist and his assistant as Irish Catholics, the crooked fire marshal as Italian, and the investigating cops as two Irishmen and an Italian, and you can see that Higgins is dealing with the major groups at each others' throats in the city of Boston. (He digs into the old-family Protestants who still control the money in other books, most emphatically in *Dreamland* and *A Choice of Enemies*.)

The Rat on Fire may look at first glance like a crime story of the police-procedural variety, but it is indeed a novel in the Mark Twain tradition of American realism. It is unflinching in its account of life in the late twentieth century in an American city and accurate in its rendition of the language its inhabitants speak. It offers neither ideological solutions for what ails the society nor sentimental hopes for its future, yet it is free of despair and of dullness. That is both an intellectual and a technical triumph, and it hinges on those arialike speeches. They put a daffy exuberance at the center of the novel, doing wonders for its pace, its tone, and finally its credibility. A character given a chance to speak doesn't make a merely reasonable, appropriate response, he unloads what is on his mind. Told that his apartment building has rats in it, Jerry Fein holds forth on how rats forced him to move his mother out of the house in Mattapan where he grew up into a home in Brookline where he is going broke paying rent and there are so few Jews that he has to shanghai Tommy Gallagher, who occasionally hires entertainers that Jerry represents, to be the tenth man when the husband of one of her friends dies. Leo Proctor doesn't merely admit to being a little stupid—"I only got an eighth-grade education and the stuff was gettin' a little hard for me the year before that"—he first celebrates in eloquent detail the stupidity that got him arrested for drunken driving in the middle of a shallow pond alongside the Massachusetts Turnpike on the Saturday night before Memorial Day, which leads him, never mind how, to the conclusion that then-President Carter is an asshole. "It's bad enough I got to be an asshole, but if the goddamned President's an asshole we are all in trouble, including poor assholes like me that can't stay out of trouble anyway, and then what the fuck we do, huh?"[5] What is on a character's mind is not always so funny. Leo Proctor on the subject of his wife's fat and Billy Malatesta on his wife's alcoholism are both appalling, and Mavis Davis's calm, grim explanation of why she can't get her son Alfred to calm down is painfully moving. It becomes all the more moving a little later when Alfred takes the three-story plunge with the fire escape.

A lot follows from Higgins's way of letting his characters talk his novel. His plots seem to grow easily out of the personalities and circumstances of his characters, though in fact those are tightly

5. Higgins, *Rat*, 18, 16.

woven plots. He doesn't have to lean on worn devices for generating suspense; he has the natural turns and rhythms of speech
to keep things moving. And—best of all—he is saved from abstraction and ideology. His characters are so deeply absorbed in themselves, even as you and I, that it never occurs to them to think
of themselves as units in a sociopolitical scheme. Even as you and
I, they think they are free to be themselves, or at least speak for
themselves.

All that talk is hard on people who have never learned to hear
what they read, a fairly numerous class these days. They can—
judging from some tin-eared reviews—follow his stories, but they
miss most of the implications and all of the fun of the arias. Then
they complain about self-indulgence and padding when a character
drifts into a diatribe on, say, the burden of having been christened
Jeremiah Francis Xavier Kennedy that concludes, "Altogether, my
father gave me four names, any one of which would persuade a reasonable man that I had a perfect reason to have killed him, but he
died before I got the chance."[6]

I don't know if Higgins's technique elicits more than ordinarily
subjective responses, but one reviewer bitterly criticized *The Mandeville Talent* because she doesn't like listening to middle-class
people from small towns in western Massachusetts. Some very
respectable reviewers can tolerate the profanity of his criminal characters but draw the line when he attributes profanity to judges, federal prosecutors, newspaper publishers, and other pillars of society.
I do not cast stones at the reviewers. My own response to *Dreamland*, a novel that some sensible people admire for its use of an un-
reliable narrator, is badly twisted by my own well-established,
carefully nurtured distaste for neurotically genteel types like that
narrator. By now, I just can't stand being in the company of such
so-and-sos, no matter how fine a job Higgins does of rendering
them. Quite possibly, the better Higgins does his kind of work the
more likely some of us in the tribe of critics are to complain about
the company he is forcing us to keep.

Still, I think it is fair to rate his two novels about Washington
politics, *A City on a Hill* and *A Year or So with Edgar*, among his least
successful because so much of the talk in them has to be about the

6. Higgins, *Kennedy for the Defense*, 15.

abstractions of national government by people whose professions place them at one end or the other of the public-relations pipeline. People who are hip-deep in actions and reactions are a lot more interesting to listen to. His later political novels, *A Choice of Enemies* and *Victories*, work better because they are grittier. *A Choice of Enemies* focuses on a man who is energetic and dangerous enough to succeed in taming the animals who inhabit the Massachusetts legislature; *Victories* focuses on a former pitcher for the Boston Red Sox living in his native Vermont, who has a natural gift for working with diverse people and who is lucky enough to have the Republican incumbent die just before a congressional election the ex-pitcher didn't have a chance of winning.

Though Higgins spent a year after he graduated from college as a student in Stanford's writing program, and though he now teaches fiction-writing workshops often enough to write a textbook for his own use *(On Writing)* he most emphatically is not an academic writer; after Stanford he was a newspaperman and before he took to teaching he was a trial lawyer, so naturally he writes for the marketplace, not the readings circuit. He cites Molière with approval: "Writing is like prostitution. First you do it for love. Then you do it for a few friends. Finally you do it for money."[7] I wouldn't take that too literally; he's out to shock students who are liable to feel that commercial considerations are beneath their delicate sensibilities. Yet he is committed to writing books that people will buy, and relatively few people will spend money on novels that don't tell an interesting story built on a good, firm plot. The trick is, of course, to manage the plot so that it doesn't throttle the rest of the novel. Most of the time he succeeds, even to the point of getting a smooth, credible ending; sometimes, though, the ending betrays him, seeming too melodramatic or too contrived. *The Patriot Game*, for example, has fine stuff about agents of the Irish Republican Army raising money in South Boston, but it climaxes in a scene that looks a little too much like the shoot-out at the end of a John Wayne movie. Similarly, though most of *Kennedy for the Defense* strikes me as tough-minded and appropriately complicated, the ending seems a trifle pat, with Jerry Kennedy coming to the rescue of his wife and daughter, who are being held captive by a young thug who has

7. Higgins, *On Writing*, 6.

invaded their home. And *Impostors*, which at heart is a challenging, engrossing morality tale, probably relies too much on a joyous bedding to take care of the complicated problems of its two main characters. Of course, these have to be counted as minor flaws; the ending is usually the most awkward and probably the least important part of a novel to get right.

Higgins regularly, almost routinely, gets the most important parts right. His characters look, sound, and act like actual human beings, and the society they are trying to survive in is every bit as complicated and infuriating as the one you and I must make do with. He doesn't preach sermons or deliver lectures. The meanings that are in his novels are deep within them, aspects of the imagined performance rather than conclusions that float to the surface of final chapters. One can almost say that his novels are all of a piece, that collectively they define a type of their own, just as one can almost say that Hemingway's short stories are all of a piece and that having any Hemingway story is better than having no Hemingway story at all. But only almost. I could get along nicely without Hemingway's story/playlet about the crucifixion, "Today Is Friday," and I still think *The Mandeville Talent* is a mistake. Higgins's novels do relate to each other in various ways, sometimes to the point of one being nearly a continuation of another (*Victories* and *Trust*, for example). Yet to read them in the sequence in which they were written is to realize that Higgins has kept pushing himself to reach farther and deeper rather than to play it safe by doing again things he has already proved he can do well.

Some reviewers, apparently, fell in love with *The Friends of Eddie Coyle* and wish he would do a lot more friends of a lot more Coyles, but Higgins is not that kind of writer. As much as I delight in *Eddie Coyle* I am grateful that he made himself go out to the end of the limb, where he could do *Wonderful Years, Wonderful Years* with its terrifyingly convincing portrait of a woman lost in paranoia; *Victories* with its much more reassuring but equally convincing portrait of a former ballplayer who found depths and abilities in himself that neither he nor anybody else knew he had; *Bomber's Law* with its Jamesian perception of how familial loyalties can work for good or for ill among both cops and criminals; *Sandra Nichols Found Dead* with its profane discovery of the qualities of goodness and mercy in such unlikely candidates as a detective-lieutenant on the verge of retiring from the state police, a judge of the probate court, and a lawyer who specializes in defending criminal cases; and *A Change of Gravity* with its clearheaded recognition of the necessary imperfections of all social institutions.

Higgins's success in recording a significant portion of the history of our times is grounded in the fullness and justness of his acceptance of the uncertainties of language, literature, and life. Actually, I think it would be correct to say that he has that "negative capability" that John Keats discovered and admired in Shakespeare, but I must admit that linking the bard of foul-mouthed Bostonians with John Keats and the Sweet Bard of Avon seems a bit odd, if not a bit much. To keep to contemporary comparisons, Higgins has a novelist's patience in the presence of diverse and even contradictory facts to see both this and that rather than a social scientist's drive to organize them to fit into a hierarchical scheme of things. Schemes, hierarchical and otherwise, are neat and easy to make thoughtful-sounding noises about, but reality is organic rather than schematic, and anyone who wishes to think effectively about it should cultivate the patience and wisdom of storytellers.

My experience with Higgins's novels illustrates, I think, some fundamental aspects of a critical reader's encounter with the uncertainties lurking on his side of the literary process. First, and most obviously, it shows the danger of hurrying to put a work in a category. Nobody who thinks Higgins's novels are crime stories can make real sense of them any more than anybody who thinks that a turnip is a piece of fresh fruit can enjoy munching on one; of course, one bite is usually enough to clear up the turnip-muncher's misapprehension, but not-very-bright reviewers have been known to plough all the way through some of Higgins's novels without realizing that they are not what the bookstores said they are. Though it's true that to do a good job of reading a novel or any other work of literature you finally need to place it, to have a sense of the kind of work it is (which is why critics need good literary educations), it is also true that you are well advised to look carefully at the thing itself before deciding what kind of thing it is. Hurrying to put a work into a category is the worst mistake a critic can make; that is why ideological criticism is so often so bad. Ideologues know before they start to read the work that if it does not conform to their ideologies it is worthless; for they have long since decided that their ideologies can't be wrong.

The next worse mistake a critic can make is to assume that the book and its author share his or her assumptions, values, and preferences. "If it looks this way to me it must look this way to everybody else." Baldly stated, that sounds preposterously naive; surely, you would think, only a very inexperienced reader could so think. But remember (in Chapter 4) Milan Kundera's savage critique of Jeffrey Meyers's reading of "Hills like White Elephants"; that's exactly the assumption Meyers, who has written several literary biographies, acted on. He is sure that Hemingway must have expected his readers to have the same politically correct sensitivities that he has. The more fully a work seems to fit your own assumptions the harder it is to back far enough off it to see the work as an independent statement. Witness how very few people can see the possibility that Shakespeare intended Shylock as a *comic* villain. "What? Do you mean that he might have thought his audience would *laugh* at Shylock's 'Hath not a Jew' soliloquy? What are you trying to do, make a Nazi of William Shakespeare? Etc. Etc." Don't tell them that there were no death camps in England in 1600, probably because there weren't more than a couple of Jews in the whole country; and especially don't remind those sensitive souls that it's always a lot of fun to see a comic villain begging to avoid getting his comeuppance. Or to take a different example—antisemitism being a very delicate subject—consider the response of contemporary feminist critics to novels, poems, and plays of earlier eras that fail to show women in the sorts of positions of authority they never held in those benighted eras. Or simply consider your own difficulty in reading past—or over or around—your own experience to respond properly to a work that seems to have come out of a quite different kind of experience. Am I, whose grandparents' names were Galligan, Hanrahan, Lawlor, and McHugh, right to nurse some nasty suspicions about T. S. Eliot just because he gave Irish names to his swinish characters? Am I distorting a poem and defaming a poet when I mutter that the Sweeneys I have known have been every bit as good as the Eliots, and mostly better company?

Actually, I think there is some considerable validity to my nasty suspicions about Eliot, but I would want a lot of strong confirmation of them before I would argue the matter in public. I would need to reexamine the poems and the essays to see if they fairly consistently demonstrate the racial, religious, and social prejudices commonly held by the class of people he grew up with, and then I would also want to cast a cold eye on the revelations contained in recent biographies. That a case could probably be made doesn't matter: my point is that I have learned—the hard way, of course—that I have to be particularly skeptical of arguments that fit my preconceptions. "What's your evidence?" That's the great question for a properly uncertain reader to pose first. Only after that has been answered can that reader begin to trust his or her opinion of the work at hand, which is finally, of course, the opinion he or she must trust. Timid, deferential readers are better than hasty, self-centered ones, but not much better.

As Milan Kundera says and as Higgins well knows, novels are highly ironic narratives. Kundera is right in arguing that therefore you have to read them slowly and more than once, but I find an apparently dizzy way of putting it more helpful: you have to read them at the pace they want to be read by you. I find that Higgins's novels are particularly good at helping me to find the right pace, because they are, in Kundera's interesting term, particularly melodic. I can't help but hear the melody of the characters' talk and, hearing it, get so fascinated by its rhythms that I don't worry about its significance. I don't know how fast or slow I am reading but I do know that I sop up the facts of the fiction long before I get around to wondering about themes or meanings. As a result, reading them combines for me—in defiance of the strictures of puritans of all stripes—a great deal of nearly mindless pleasure and some exceedingly useful intellectual discipline.

7

The Dimension of the Past

All of the novels of George V. Higgins are set in the present. They may look back in one way or another to events in a character's past, but it is almost always the personal and usually the relatively recent past so that the reader never loses sight of its connection with the events in the present that are the novel's major concern. That is to say, Higgins really is focused on the social rather than the political or intellectual history of his time—on the lives people lived rather than on the forces and events that washed over their lives—as are most, though not all, Twainian realists. It's not that he and the writers he grew up admiring share Henry Ford's belief that "history is bunk," it's that history is too abstract for them. They are too intensely involved in what they can see, touch, taste, smell, hear to have much trust or even interest in any but the most concrete remnants of the past. Realizing that if they are to have any chance of getting the history of our time right, they have to trust facts, not ideas and certainly not ideologies, they simply are not equipped by temperament or training to respond to the pull of the vanished past. Higgins couldn't *know* Puritan Boston or Civil War Boston or even late-nineteenth-century Boston the way he *knows* the Boston of his time, and like a lot of other good Americans, he devoutly believes in the importance of knowing what you are talking about. Historical novels are not for him—I doubt that he would trust even *War and Peace* enough to read it all the way through.

Mary Lee Settle shares important ideas and attitudes with Higgins: she, too, is a realist of an emphatically American, if not quite so precisely a Twainian, sort; she, too, distrusts ideologies and despises ideologues while valuing people who know what they are talking about and do something about it; and she is as much—as incorrigibly—a novelist as he is. But she cannot avoid history—the

131

past may be for her the most important context in which to place human beings if you are to understand them—and she has a strong, though unprogrammatic, belief in the illuminating power of myths. She and Higgins both believe individuality and freedom are facts of life, but when she set out to understand for herself their link with violence in American life she wound up writing a quintet of novels that began with the story of two troopers in Cromwell's army in the middle of the seventeenth century and didn't get into present time until the last book. I can't imagine Higgins ever wanting to write a book that could be described as a biography of a place, but Settle, who had found important themes and material for her work as well as badly needed support for herself in Turkey, expressed her gratitude in *Turkish Reflections: A Biography of a Place*, a book that deals with the remarkable capacity of the people who live on that very rugged piece of land to keep traces of several millennia of their past alive in their ways of thinking and being. Naturally, she hasn't fared much better than Higgins has with the people who deal out labels: *Turkish Reflections* got reviewed as a travel book and *The Beulah Quintet* was for a while dimly perceived as belonging in the same category as historical novels of the heaving-bosoms school.

Settle's way of working with history is both distinctive and important, but before going into a detailed consideration of it I should give a rough account of her career. She began with a fierce burst of work: three novels published in three years. The first one published, *The Love Eaters* (1954), was actually written after *The Kiss of Kin* (1955), and she was hard at work on the third one, *O Beulah Land* (1956), before either of them appeared in print. *The Kiss of Kin* strikes me as the sort of thing that a very bright, very clever writer who is pushing to make up for the time she lost to the war has to get out of her system before she is ready to do her own kind of work. *The Love Eaters*, the second novel she wrote though the first one published, started out to be another bright young stunt, the product of a bet that if the story of Phaedra were done in a modern setting the audience would not recognize her as a tragic figure, only as comic, pathetic, even menopausal. She won the bet, but much more importantly, in the course of creating a realistic modern setting for her Phaedra in Canona, a city modeled on Charleston, West Virginia, Settle discovered her own pressing, complex material. It doesn't look like much, just a spoiled brat coming home for Christmas from her freshman year at college and dreading the prospect of spending two weeks with her fiercely genteel mother and her kindly, bumbling father in their elaborately nice house. But the scene with Sally Bea, first in the train and then in her parents' car, jumps with life in the way in which no merely clever fiction can, and the niceness of her parents' way of life in Canona turns out to be both the cause and the product of more and of more different kinds of violence than can be dealt with in a subplot. Settle promptly dove headfirst in rash American fashion into a remarkably unmodish project, a series of historical novels on the roots of that violence and that gentility. She thought that she had a trilogy on her hands and that it could begin with a novel on the period just prior to the Revolutionary War when the area around Charleston was first settled by whites. She took her title, *O Beulah Land*, from the title of a revivalist hymn on a Burl Ives album, "I look away across the sea, where mansions are prepared for me, and view the shining glory shore, my heaven, my home forevermore." The land hunger that she heard in that hymn was the first clue, she says, to guide her into a vivid, fictionally valid sense of the people she needed to write about.

O Beulah Land is a still fresh, very attractive, remarkably assured piece of work; *Know Nothing* (1960), the second part of the projected trilogy, is every bit as good but less immediately attractive because it is dealing with the dark, turbid years just before the outbreak of the Civil War. With two novels as strong as those behind her, Settle must have felt that she was riding high; if so, she was brought back to earth and flattened when her attempt to bring the trilogy to completion, *Fight Night on a Sweet Saturday* (1964), turned out to be a disaster. Eventually she realized that that "dead failure" was "the most painful and the best thing that could have happened" because it forced her to realize that her trilogy had to be a quintet, starting earlier and extending through two full novels, dealing with material she had tried to cram into one in *Fight Night*. In the meantime she dug in her heels and kept on working. If she couldn't do the big job of comprehending the witches' brew of gentility, piety, violence, and love of freedom that characterizes American culture in general and the culture of the upper South in particular, she damn well could do the smaller one of looking at how she managed to get out from under her own long training in expensive gentility to become a serious woman and writer. First came *All the Brave Promises* (1966), a memoir of her wartime service in Britain's Women's Auxiliary Air Force, in which she had enlisted after the American armed forces rejected her for poor eyesight. That experience taught her, among many other things, to despise the officer class and to identify with what the British call with snobbish disdain the "other ranks" at the bottom of the military chain of command. After writing a juvenile, *The Story of Flight* (1967), to keep the pot boiling, she went back to the crucial experience at Sweet Briar College that led her at the end of her sophomore year to strike out on her own path rather than the one her family had picked for her. Though *The Clam Shell* (1971) started out to be another memoir, it turned into a novel about a girl for whom an attempted rape became a springboard into freedom. She is merely disgusted with the lout she dated and with her own stupid, prudish self, but she is furious at all of the ladylike students and officials at "Nelson-Page College" who both envy and blame her for having had a sexual experience. The book ends with a scene Jean Renoir would have admired: the heroine and the one powerful teacher she has had are laughing uproariously at the end of the college's "traditional" May Day ceremonies—"celebration of fertility by a group of perpetual virgins." He has broken away by having a nervous breakdown; she by enduring the attempted rape. Both plainly feel that their freedom would have been cheap at twice the price.

The Clam Shell is a fine novel that almost ruined Settle's career. Its publisher, Seymour Lawrence, apparently took a dislike to it; he wrapped it in a magnolia-covered dust jacket and released it as quietly as possible. She looked for a while like a writer a publisher couldn't afford to publish, yet it is now clear that she had become a mature novelist in full command of her very considerable powers. Work on another juvenile, *The Scopes Trial* (1972), forced her to think about the motto of the American Civil Liberties Union that was taken from Jack Lilbourne's speech to the Star Chamber in 1632, "For what is done to any one may be done to every one . . . "; that in turn drove her to study the period, its language, and its ideas about democracy. She published *Prisons* in 1973, the first volume in what she now realized had to be a five-volume set. With that remarkable novel behind her, she was off and running. In the next dozen years she wrote *Blood Tie* (1977), *The Scapegoat* (1980), *The Killing Ground* (1982), and *Celebration* (1986). The first and fourth of these deal with her experience as an American abroad, *Blood Tie* being set almost entirely in Turkey and *Celebration* mostly in Turkey, Africa, and London. *The Scapegoat* is a full treatment of the material on the mine wars that she had tried to deal with quickly in *Fight Night on a Sweet Saturday; The Killing Ground* is a full and fully successful reworking of the material in that failed novel that deals with modern Canona. *Charley Bland* (1989) stands apart from the *Quintet,* but it deals with modern Canona and with characters that have appeared in novels from *The Love Eaters* on. It seems to hover between fiction and autobiography, as *The Love Eaters* did and as *The Clam Shell* did. In 1991 she went even farther out along the borders separating genres and published *Turkish Reflections: A Biography of a Place. Choices* (1995) comes back squarely to the novel form; though at first glance it looks like an autobiographical summing up, it is a thoroughly fictional product of a veteran's slightly dopey experience of suddenly realizing that here she is now and she can look all the way back to then and God knows she never expected that to happen. That's "slightly dopey" because she has spent almost her entire career insisting on the necessity of placing human beings in their historical context in order to understand them; apparently she sort of forgot to notice that while she was getting her work done she was subject to historical changes, too.

Settle has given a very interesting account of the writing of the *Quintet* in an essay that appeared in *The Southern Review* and that Scribner's printed as a pamphlet to accompany a boxed set of the five novels, "The Search for Beulah Land." The search started, she says, "with an image, strong enough to act as memory. . . . Like a dream image, it was subjective, sensuous, mysterious," and it kept her at work for twenty-eight years. "There were two men in a drunk tank on a Saturday night in West Virginia. They were strangers to each other. One hit the other and he fell. That was all. But within the image was the violence, the choice of one stranger over another among mindless men on a Saturday night, their anger or their sorrow released by drink. It stayed with me as an unresolved memory stays and demands answers to questions. What past was behind the fist, what old prejudice, what new anger? Then I asked of the image one essential question, a question without an answer—why?"[1]

1. Mary Lee Settle, "The Search for Beulah Land: The Story behind *The Beulah Quintet*," 3.

Through twenty-eight years the question kept nagging at her and she kept coming back to it. She realized early on that she had to strip herself of romantic, nostalgic notions of her region's history and somehow get far enough back in time to find out for herself "why one man hit another in a drunk tank on a Saturday night." The years just before the Revolution when the frontier of the Allegheny mountains was "slowly and illegally" opening seemed like the right place to start. Her problem as she understood it when she began work on *O Beulah Land* in the reading room of the British Museum (the warmest place to work in the London of 1954) was to make a vivid sense of that time and place part of her own memory. Not her knowledge, her memory, for she wanted to write a novel, not a monograph.

She plunged into reading within the century to create a historic memory she did not have. From the beginning she was careful not to read "reliable" nineteenth- and twentieth-century accounts of the period; she didn't need to know what actually happened, say, at Braddock's defeat by the French and Indian forces, only what the people of the time thought had happened. She was also careful not to take notes on what she read, for fear that she would remember the notes and the books instead of the places and events they talked about. The British Museum turned out, somewhat unexpectedly, to be the perfect place for her to work because it had on its shelves hundreds of long-forgotten contemporary accounts of the settlement of her region that taught her not only what the people of the time thought but also, and possibly more importantly, the language in which they talked and wrote about what they thought. An ear for the language is as crucial to Settle's novels, historical or contemporary, as it is to Higgins's accounts of the byways, both legal and illegal, of his Boston. She was careful not to go beyond 1774 in her reading for *O Beulah Land* because she realized that in a time of crisis such as the American Revolution "language changes and grows and diminishes so quickly that a phrase used in 1775 could be wrong in the mouth of someone in this country in 1774."[2]

A passion for accuracy of detail, especially, or at least most strikingly, sensory detail, is just as crucial. Living in London she had to call up a full awareness of the mountain country where she had

2. Ibid., 9.

been born and raised from her own deep past and from observations she had never consciously made. She went to the zoo. "There, in the caged animals, were hints of feral lives, some aids to the memory of isolation and fear which comes, not from being lost in cities, but in a world of indifference whether . . . of trees or men. I watched the puma, day after day, with its wild familiar agate eyes. I watched the hair part on the grey squirrel's back as it moved and fed. I watched the eagles, their arrogant little eyes. Because intellectual memory was not enough, I drank two glasses of gin for courage and went into the bear pit to feel the pelts of the native American brown bears. I made no choices; there was no mental editing, only the guidance of the place they had come from, as if they knew, and I had forgotten, what it was to be so free that there was only the prison of watchfulness left, day and night, as in a wild animal. I knew I had seen these things before, but all of that had been long ago."[3]

Settle's historical novels are in no danger of lapsing into abstraction—two glasses of gin and the feel of the pelts of the bears in their pit would, I think, give lifetime immunity to that disease. Nonetheless, the novels of the *Quintet* are grounded in concepts as well as in images. Just as important as the image of the fight in the drunk tank to the entire work is the conceptual realization that a propensity for violence and a love of freedom are permanently intertwined in the American psyche. *Prisons* is a particularly clear illustration. She knew, as the failure of *Fight Night on a Sweet Saturday* sank in, that she had to do a quintet rather than a trilogy and that it had to start earlier in time than the 1770s. Reading Jack Lilbourne's speech to the Star Chamber in 1632 led her to the realization that somewhere in that tumultuous time she might find the source of the political language of freedom that had been eluding her. A lot of reading, a lot of research followed, but she could not begin to write her novel until on a weekend with friends in Burford, England, she found— and put her fingers into—bullet holes in the churchyard wall where the men who refused to obey the order to go fight the Irish in Ireland were shot on April 14, 1649.[4] *Prisons* is an extraordinary piece of storytelling. The narrator is a twenty-year-old trooper in Cromwell's army; yet Settle so thoroughly masters his language and so

3. Ibid., 9–10.
4. Ibid., 14.

convincingly demonstrates his perceptions that one forgets to be impressed by this performance across the lines of gender and of three centuries.

Settle has achieved a body of work that is coherent and ambitious; it is also distinctive. Everything she has written, even *The Kiss of Kin*, is unmistakably her own and no one else's. In or out of the *Quintet*, working within or outside of Canona material, set in mid-seventeenth-century England or in London at the time of the moon landing, it all bears her stamp. Yet there is nothing showily idiosyncratic about it. She keeps her language close to the language her characters use and her fictional techniques appropriate to the texture of the lives they live. She is like certain great actors who seem to live in their parts rather than act in them. She has her alter egos, of course, but she can enter as surely into the character of the richest, most powerful man in a small port city in Turkey or a nineteenth-century evangelical Protestant woman from Ohio who has married into a slaveholding family in Virginia or a seven-foot African Jesuit as into a woman raised in prosperous gentility in Charleston, West Virginia, in the 1930s. Neither self-assertive nor self-effacing, she is so intent on the world that is out there that she doesn't have much time to worry about the self within. She is the polar opposite of a narcissist; that in itself would make her an imposing presence in our time.

One cannot define the individuality of an artist of any size. But since she insists that each of her novels arises as *Prisons* did from the joining of an image and a concept perhaps an image from *All the Brave Promises* and a concept from *Celebration* can join to evoke some sense of what makes a Settle novel so plainly a Settle novel.

In September 1942, Settle boarded a ship in New York to go to London in order to enlist in the WAAF. She believed in the causes for which the war was being fought; apparently she also believed that she had as much right to go to the war as anybody did. Fine. But nothing in her life had prepared her to swallow easily the humiliations routinely visited upon enlisted personnel in any military organization or to fit smoothly into a company consisting largely of seventeen-year-old girls from the East End of London. She was coming back to the barracks one night when a group of the girls grabbed her as she stepped through the blackout curtain and threw her like a sack of grain into a large puddle in the mud at the foot of the steps. They stood in the doorway jeering at her—"That'll teach the fuckin' toffee-nose." She promptly did some teaching of her own: "Out of me rumbled a fury all the way from Morgan's raiders and a language I didn't know I knew. I just lay there on the ground and swore until there was a dead silence."[5] Plainly, she was not a fuckin' toffee-nose; nor were they the sheep she had thought they were. She still identifies herself with them, for *All the Brave Promises: Memories of Aircraft Woman 2nd Class 2146391* is dedicated to "the wartime other ranks of the Women's Auxiliary Air Force, Royal Air Force—below the rank of sergeant."

That scene tells a lot about Settle, who was glad to serve in the WAAF but couldn't bring herself to swear an oath of allegiance to the King of England. She is an American, specifically southern American, a descendant of the people who served in Morgan's raiders during the Civil War and capable, to her surprise, of speaking their most pungent language. Seize her in the dark, throw her on her back in the mud, and jeer at her, and she gives way to rage, not to self-pity. She simply does not believe in feeling sorry for herself. Her books are full of people of a sort one would rather not have to admit any kinship with—murderers, slaveholders, cowards, drunks, shady CIA agents, strikebreakers, unfaithful husbands, promiscuous wives, religious bigots, homosexual leeches, and macho sadists—but the only ones a reader is authorized to treat as strangers and with contempt are those who feel sorry for themselves. Her most savage comment on the rich, spoiled ladies of Canona is that "they are, in one of the bloodiest centuries of the Christian era, women to whom nothing has happened that is not personal. Aging, dry, and complicated girls, they still call each other girls, weathered by years, unchanged."[6] They are so tightly focused on themselves that they have no room left to feel pity over what life and the world have done to others.

I would link the image of Aircraft Woman 2nd Class Settle flat on her back in the mud spouting curses rather than going boohoo with the motivating concept of *Celebration* that she states as its epigraph: "The real knowledge of death is sudden and certain. It takes different people different ways. After that crossing to the less

5. Settle, *All the Brave Promises*, 36.
6. Settle, *The Killing Ground*, 9.

naive side of the river Styx, stripped of the useless armor of blindness, nothing is taken for granted. Objects are more defined. Colors are brighter. People know this who have been in wars."

Settle herself has crossed the Styx more than once. She went to the war. Though she was not in combat she had ample experience of the terror of being bombed, by planes and by missiles, and she earned a medical discharge from the WAAF by spending far too many hours with a headset on trying to ignore the noise of the German's jamming of radio frequencies in order to guide damaged English planes back to their bases. She also endured the terror of a serious bout with cancer, just as Teresa Cerrutti, the heroine of *Celebration* has. Teresa's private little postoperative ritual was probably her own: she took off "the ruffledom menopausal pink peignoir" her mother had given her, cut it into small pieces, and stood in the kitchen naked "with an angry red line from her navel to where her pubic hair had been," determined to get on with the rest of her life.[7]

That knowledge of what life looks like from the other side of the Styx can account for a lot in Settle's life and work. It alone would have made it impossible for her ever to have settled for the comforts of life as one of the girls; at the same time it forced her to acknowledge just how tempting those comforts were. She has gone deeper, I think, than any other American writer into the destructive nature of the genteel life, but she is not so silly as to deny the attractions of its appurtenances. Nor is she silly enough to recoil from gentility into ideology. That's for green boys and girls who want new fairy tales to replace the ones Mommy and Daddy told them. On the other side of the river, *-ist* and *-ism* words don't make much sense; you can't use them to separate sheep from goats or to tell yourself anything useful about how to live the rest of your life.

Mortality, then, is one of the fundamental themes of Settle's novels. She doesn't land flush on it until *Celebration*, but you can't write novels like *The Beulah Quintet* without realizing that those who are born must die and without embracing something like Ecclesiastes' view of the passing of the generations. *Prisons* ends with the two central characters, Thankful Perkins and Jonathan Church, standing up to the firing squad, still affirming the rightness of what they have done; *Blood Tie* ends with the brutal murder of a young man

7. Settle, *Celebration*, 9.

by a Fascist policeman, which has the effect of cutting the knots in his younger brother's mind that had rendered him mute for most of his life. All of the novels support the forceful summary of the theme that Settle gives in *Celebration* in the form of a speech by Teresa's friend Noel on the night of her wedding. He has recognized that one way or another most of the people who have gathered to celebrate her wedding have themselves crossed the River Styx. "Something has to happen," he says, "you can't retreat from." For himself it is the experience of having to live without knowing whether the great love of his life, a Chinese boy he met in Hong Kong, is dead or alive. "So what are we left with? All that we know is that we must love, hard as it is, and we, not other people this time, but we, lovely us, must die. All we can do for one another finally is to do both of those things gracefully, and with as little fuss as possible, so as— how is it said in wartime?—not to frighten the others unduly."[8]

For Settle, as for a great many people whose thinking has a religious dimension, mortality makes love both possible and necessary. Her mind as well as her temperament compel her to confront life with hope and to accept its blessings, as she so emphatically does in *Choices,* without guilt. In literary-critical circles that is a decidedly unfashionable attitude, but she has long since gotten accustomed to being out of fashion. Actually, as I have been arguing throughout this book, the resolutely gloomy critics and theorists are the ones who are becoming old hat.

From *The Beulah Quintet* on, all of Settle's works combine lucid intelligence with a deep sensitivity to language and to images. They are simultaneously dreamy and purposeful, mythic and rationalistic, assuaging and astringent. *Celebration,* for example, is powered by a clearheaded determination to explore the nature of survival, but it lies, according to Settle, between two images, one of a woman alone making a list, the other of a small group of people in London observing the anniversary of the death of King Charles I. The result is a potent novel, the work of a Hemingway who has survived cancer in the uterus rather than shrapnel in the knee and who trusts what she has learned in the reading room of the British Museum as much as what she has learned in beds, barracks, and bars. Or turn the emphasis around: it's the work of a woman who has had the

8. Ibid., 344–45.

sense to learn a great deal from Hemingway—from Conrad and Stendhal and other masters of uncertainty, too—and the integrity to insist on going her own way as a writer and a person.

Though you don't hear the matter discussed very much, their intelligence is a tricky matter for both novelists and novel-readers to manage. Too muscular, too unrestrained, too proud an intelligence in either reader or writer will make a hash of any novel, no matter how promising its material; but a weak, dull, conventional intelligence in either reader or writer is guaranteed to produce nothing but weak, dull, conventional results. Writers who either are or fancy themselves to be brilliant intellectuals cannot manage that submissiveness to story that's essential to novels any more than students who boast of their high grade point averages can believe that a mere story can be smarter than they are. Settle, Higgins, and Skvorecky, like all of the other novelists I have touched on in this book, possess first-class minds, but as novelists they keep those minds firmly in their place. Skvorecky identifies so strongly with his unglamorous, unpretentious characters and is so whimsically suspicious of anything bearing official approval that many of the people who review his books don't notice how sophisticated they are with respect to technique. Higgins buries himself so deeply in his novels that he doesn't seem so much to be telling a story as letting his characters talk it; when one of his books is hitting on all cylinders the talk is so outrageously energetic and absorbing that any thought of what he has on his mind would seem like a pointless interruption. Settle lets her intelligence be seen; she has to, for a concept is always one of the armatures a novel of hers is built on. But since an image is always the other armature neither she nor her reader can see the novel as anything remotely like an exercise in conceptual thinking. To put it another way, though she has the intellectual capacity to do and to analyze a great deal of original research she has no interest in being seen as anything other than a storyteller. Robertson Davies, to whom I want to turn next, had a flashier mind and chose a more flamboyant way of dealing with it, as befitted a man who stood well over six feet, had a long white beard, and wore a scarlet cape.

I feel a bit simpleminded admitting that I didn't start reading Robertson Davies until after his eighth novel, *What's Bred in the Bone,* was published in this country in 1985. Not only had seven good novels preceded it, they were all of a sort I like and I had been complaining that such very novelish novels were in disgracefully short supply. Fortunately, Davies is gentle with the simpleminded; indeed, he so despises the excesses of rationalism that he passes himself off as simpleminded, too—or at least as silly enough to love the old melodramas and to have some belief in magic, ghosts, devils, angels, and supernatural claptrap in general. I am further comforted by two books of criticism that were published almost simultaneously with his ninth novel, *The Lyre of Orpheus* (1988), *The Company We Keep* (1988) by Wayne Booth and *The Call of Stories* (1989) by Robert Coles. Both Booth and Coles portray themselves as somewhat simpleminded, or at least humble minded, and their books very strongly suggest that only those who are not impressed with themselves can enter the worlds created by great novels. Insufferably brilliant people may well be barred at the gates.

If I (like most American critics) was slow getting around to reading Davies's novels, he was unusually slow in getting around to writing them. He was thirty-eight when his first novel was published—*Tempest-Tost* (1951)[9]—and eighty-one when his eleventh and last one, *The Cunning Man* (1994), came out a few months before he died. He wasn't only a novelist; he had substantial careers in the theater, in journalism, and in academia. As a man of the theater he worked under Tyrone Guthrie at the Old Vic until the war forced its closing, helped to establish and run the Shakespeare Festival Theatre at Stratford, Ontario (again in association with Guthrie), and wrote a dozen and a half or so plays that were generally well received in Canada, though not in New York and London where theatrical reputations are made. As a newspaperman he was editor of the *Examiner* in Peterborough, Ontario, through most of the forties and fifties; he also did a lot of reviewing and writing for magazines in that period. As an academic with a degree from Oxford he flourished through the sixties and seventies in the University of Toronto as Professor of Drama and as Master of Massey College.

No wonder his novels stand apart from most American ones of the last thirty or forty years. By the time he got started he was too old and too busy to write about the pangs of adolescence; he had

9. Here and in the following paragraphs the year given in parentheses is the year of original publication, which is not necessarily the same as the year of publication of the edition cited in the bibliography.

spent too many years in positions of authority and responsibility to play the outcast; and as a successful scholar and administrator he couldn't very well do the anti-intellectual bit, either. Steamy sexuality was out, too. How could a man who wears a long white beard and who was married to the same woman for more than fifty years strike sexpot poses on his dustjackets? You could say that he had little choice but to write as a grown-up who knows and is amused by the ways of the world.

Until his last few years Davies wrote his novels in sets of three, first publishing each novel separately and sometime later gathering them into trilogies. The first set consists of *Tempest-Tost, Leaven of Malice* (1954), and *A Mixture of Frailties* (1958), collectively known as *The Salterton Trilogy* and first published as a single volume in 1986. (*Tempest-Tost* is the only one of his novels that was not promptly published in this country as well as in Canada. *Leaven of Malice* is the only one that he has ever adapted for the stage; that play, in turn, is the only one of his ever to be given a New York production.) The second set consists of *Fifth Business* (1970), *The Manticore* (1972), and *World of Wonders* (1975); it was published in a single volume as *The Deptford Trilogy* in 1983. The third set consists of *The Rebel Angels* (1981), *What's Bred in the Bone* (1985), and *The Lyre of Orpheus* (1988); it was published in a single volume in 1991 as *The Cornish Trilogy*.

Each set is distinctly different from the others. *The Salterton Trilogy* is the lightest, gayest, most loosely strung of the three. *The Deptford Trilogy* traces the complicated consequences of a simple, commonplace act—one boy throwing a snowball with a stone in its center at another boy—and focuses in an intellectually disciplined way on Carl Jung's ideas about the role of myths in human affairs. *The Cornish Trilogy* is more ramshackle, more openly arbitrary in its planning, as though by now Davies no longer felt the need to worry about the niceties of novel writing. In their different ways all are comedies. Loving comedies of all sorts, I myself would have trouble ranking one set ahead of another; distrusting comedies as so many of them do, American critics are likely to prefer *The Deptford Trilogy* because it works carefully with ideas that the solemn can consider "worth" studying.

The Salterton Trilogy begins and ends with theatrical material, an amateur group's production of *The Tempest* and a highly professional production of a new opera; in between, in *Leaven of Malice*, the material is journalistic, but newspapers being of necessity a species of theater the difference is more apparent than real. I think that anyone coming across this trilogy cold, so to speak, would feel that the novelist who wrote it had been influenced to an unusual extent by dramatists, perhaps especially by George Bernard Shaw. Davies's own plays, such as the three gathered in *Hunting Stuart and Other Plays*, do seem Shavian, offering generous quantities of amusing talk and taking pleasure in prankish but instructive turns of plot. But the *Salterton* novels are so free of intellectual pretensions and of malice that I see more in them of an earlier Irish playwright, Richard Brinsley Sheridan, than of Shaw. I see even more of that playwright who was forced to become a novelist, Henry Fielding. Indeed, I think that in this trilogy, Davies is closer to Fielding than any other twentieth-century novelist I know of. In tone, plot, and narrative technique, and especially in the easy, unassuming intelligence of the work as a whole, the novels remind me of *Joseph Andrews* and *Tom Jones*. Davies relishes the obstinacy with which the minor characters in *Tempest-Tost* cling to their most ridiculous traits, puts a joke at the center of the plot of *Leaven of Malice* (a maliciously false notice of their engagement brings together two people who really should and who finally do marry each other), and demonstrates in *A Mixture of Frailties* the intricate but sure way a talented girl can grow into the gifted woman she needs to be. In short, he generates a kind of laughter Fielding would approve of.

The Deptford Trilogy is something of a tour de force. *Fifth Business* draws its title from theatrical history (the player in old-fashioned drama and opera companies who regularly acted the part of the character who was neither hero, heroine, confidante, nor villain but who was essential to bring about the denouement was often referred to as "Fifth Business") but in narrative method and structure it is pretty much what you would expect of a novel tracing the history of the relationship between two men who were boys together in a small town in Canada. Though it has some startling, even bizarre things in it, they are muted by the tone of the work as a whole. *The Manticore* is a far less conventional novel, for it is almost purely an account of a Jungian analysis, according to competent judges a very sound, though of course condensed account. The narrator of *Fifth Business* is Dunstan Ramsay, who is retiring as Senior History Master at a prestigious Canadian school; the narrator of *The Manticore* is the son of Ramsay's childhood friend, who is sick with guilt after his father's death in an automobile accident that was probably a suicide. Ramsay is again the narrator in *World of Wonders*, but now he is the friend and associate of a world-famous magician, and the story he tells is wild stuff. Yet everything in all three of these very different novels follows from the moment Boy Staunton threw a rock-filled snowball at Dunstan Ramsay, who ducked so that it hit a pregnant woman by mistake. Everything in all three of these novels also contributes to Davies's exploration of Jungian concepts. It is a most successful piece of intellectual exploration, perhaps because long before he wrote the novels Davies read all of Freud and of Jung—by the standards of our breezier "psychological" novelists and critics, that is almost a species of cheating. Certainly he gets much deeper into Jung's ideas than most literary critics have. They tend to rest happily when they have reduced complex works to simple myths; he is never reductive. Rather, he shows how the myths manifest themselves in the complexities of human behavior, both individual and collective, permeating our minds, becoming both the basic structures of our understanding and the boundaries of our freedom. By the time he is finished even someone as skeptical as I have been has to admit that the Jungian approach makes a lot of good sense, particularly as a means of resisting the tyranny of Descartian rationalism.

Yet Davies insists that he is not an intellectual. When people used to claim that he was an existentialist he always denied it on the grounds that though he had had existentialism explained to him many times the explanations never made enough sense to him "to cling." He describes himself as "scrappily educated" and not very good at thinking. What thinking he does always comes later as he is trying to figure out what to do with what he has experienced or intuited.[10] His theatrical experience largely preceded his reading of Freud and Jung; thus *World of Wonders* is packed full of theatrical lore and it serves as the basis for understanding, not for illustrating, Jungian ideas.

10. Donald Cameron, *Conversations with Canadian Novelists, Part 1*, 41–42.

The central character in the novel, the child who was born prematurely when that woman was struck by the snowball Dunstan Ramsay ducked, tells in a long section (in effect, a first-person narrative inside Ramsay's first-person narrative) of his theatrical apprenticeship to one of the last of the great nineteenth-century actor-managers, Sir John Tresize. Magnus, who had been a trickster on the very edge of society, transformed himself into a hero, albeit of an odd sort, by playing Sir John's double in *Scaramouche, The Master of Ballantrae,* and other popular melodramas during a crisscrossing tour of Canada. By playing the double—that is, by making a fierce effort to get inside the skin of somebody apparently identical with but actually opposite to himself—Magnus worked something like a Jungian cure of his own crippled psyche, and the melodramas themselves taught him fundamental truths about the nature of human affairs that he had been too set apart to have a chance to learn.

Davies plainly shares his character's respect for the great nineteenth-century actors and for the melodramas they played in. That will strike most nicely educated readers of *World of Wonders* as decidedly odd. No doubt many tell themselves that he doesn't really mean it. But he really, truly does admire those old melodramas that most of us dismiss as ridiculous. He makes that explicitly clear in the Alexander Lectures for 1982. The melodramas are coarse stuff, he says, but "theatre is a coarse art. It is coarse as music is coarse; it appeals immediately to primary, not secondary elements in human nature, and if drama and music can not grab you with a fine strong effect, all the elaboration of intellectual art will go for nothing."[11] The melodramas do hold a mirror up to nature, a mirror in which everything is much larger than life-size, and therefore a mirror in which even the nearsighted can make out the lineaments of their lives. Badly acted, shabbily produced, or poorly read (few of us can do a good job of reading even the most familiar sort of play) they are indeed ridiculous. Properly done—that is, with skillful actors trained to play the flamboyant with the right touch of restraint, and for an audience that doesn't care how naive it might look as long as it gains full expression of its emotions—they are powerful works of art. Low, coarse art, that is.

11. Robertson Davies, *The Mirror of Nature,* 46.

Davies knows he is right because he is old enough to have seen good productions of many of the melodramas, and also because he has carefully studied the history of the nineteenth-century theater. I know he is right because I once had the good luck to see a fine, funny production at the Abbey Theatre in Dublin of *Arrah-na-Pogue, or The Wicklow Wedding* by Dion Boucicault, but also because I have paid a lot of attention to the early film comedians, all of whom had been soaked in the theater of melodrama. (For a highly instructive example, watch Ernest Torrance and Buster Keaton portray father and son in *Steamboat Bill, Jr.*) In a pinch, the cover of the paperback edition of *The Mirror of Nature* will all by itself go a long way towards justifying Davies's opinion of melodrama. It is a photograph, printed in magenta tones, of Sarah Bernhardt as Mrs. Clarkson in *The Stranger.* She is standing next to an ornately carved piece of furniture, her right arm resting on it, not leaning on it, for the posture of her body is much too alert and elegant to be described as dependent on anything for support. She is wearing a beautiful, elaborate, flowing, entirely ladylike gown, but her long black gloves and the riding crop carelessly held in her hands are not so ladylike, at least not so sweetly so. She has, of course, a hauntingly beautiful face, and she is looking directly into the camera with the coolest, calmest, most knowledgeable stare imaginable. Anyone—man or woman—who wouldn't be moved by even this single photograph to admiration of what a great actress could convey in a good melodrama is seriously deficient in ways that it would be impolite to specify.

Sensible writers make compromises by the dozen in order to bring their readers along with them all the way through their books; for they know that writers need readers more than readers need writers. Being a very sensible writer, Davies takes good care of his readers in the Frank Cornish series as he did in the first two trilogies; it's just that now he is willing to bounce us around a little harder. He hasn't bothered cushioning the turns of the plot with transitions, forecasts, explanations, and so forth; nor has he softened the oddities of his characters and of his own way of thinking. Instead of easing into Jungian ideas via the comments of a psychoanalyst from the Jung Institute, he takes them as givens, as the lumber, so to speak, with which he can make the parts of a highly comic melodrama. In *The Deptford Trilogy* he merely flirted with belief in the supernatural—a woman whom Dunstan Ramsay believes is responsible for saintly miracles, and a master of theatrical magic who may also command some less explicable kind of magic. But in *The Cornish Trilogy* he is not nearly so maybeish. In *The Rebel Angels* the gypsy-mother of the heroine does some potent things with a pack of Tarot cards: we don't have to believe in the literal truth of the rituals with the cards, but he does not give us any handy rational way out. He employs supernatural narrators (the Lesser Zadkiel, angel of biography, and the Daimon Maimas) in parts of *What's Bred in the Bone;* and in *The Lyre of Orpheus* the spirit of E. T. A. Hoffman comments from limbo on the efforts to complete and produce the opera he was writing when he died. He gets so much fine comedy out of these supernatural observers that he doesn't need to bother with the question of whether you "really" believe in the supernatural. Suit yourself; explanations and "real" truths no longer seem very important to Davies.

In all sorts of respects the Frank Cornish novels are more extravagant than the earlier ones. Take the matter of sex. Though Davies has never had any interest in writing erotica, at least he was willing to attribute to his characters sexual behavior of the ordinary but enjoyable sort. In *A Mixture of Frailties,* for example, Monica Gall's attachment to Giles Revelstoke may be foolish (because he is intensely selfish) but it is thoroughly understandable—that is, she has a wonderful time in bed with him. The carnal connections we hear about in the Frank Cornish novels are mostly dully unattractive, essentially accidental couplings in which at least one of the participants is not really quite aware of what is going on. The one scene of delight is a lesbian one in *The Lyre of Orpheus:* an older, experienced woman slips into the bathtub with the surly young genius who is to complete Hoffman's opera and scrubs her in unexpected ways and places. Then and later, the two enjoy themselves greatly; the narrative, however, mostly stresses what a good thing it is for Hulda Schnakenburg that somebody was teaching her to wash frequently and to take pleasure in herself (even somebody with the god-awful, antierotic name of Gunilla Dahl-Soot). The plot of *The Rebel Angels* requires a dose of masculine perversion near the end so that two dabblers in evil will destroy each other. He must have gotten it out of Kraft-Ebbing; few readers will find anything enticing about having several yards of folded ribbon slowly pulled out of the rectum.

Davies treats all of the elements of the Frank Cornish novels in the same self-assured, amused way. Wanting for his heroine a solid foothold in a culture that has little respect for rational views, he gives her a mother who is a Gypsy with strong psychic gifts. Needing, in *The Rebel Angels*, a brilliant scientist who will pursue ideas wherever they lead him, he offers us Ozy Froats, who has followed his hunches about the connection between body types and personality into a scientifically careful study of human feces. Needing, in *What's Bred in the Bone*, to link Frank Cornish with the centers of power in the modern world, he makes him a rich man who hides his position in British military intelligence behind a career in the art world as an expert restorer, critic, and—occasionally—forger of late medieval paintings.

But the huge, thumping extravagance is the one at the center of *The Lyre of Orpheus:* Arthur Cornish, Frank's nephew and heir, decides that the first benefaction of the Cornish Foundation will be to support a Ph.D. candidate's completion of the opera that E. T. A. Hoffman left in fragments at his death and then to sponsor a full-scale production of it. The title of the opera is *Arthur of Britain, or The Magnanimous Cuckold*. Sure enough, at the end of the novel Arthur of Canada is a cuckold, magnanimously accepting as his own a child that he could not have sired. Of course, the Canadian Arthur's story is the stuff of comic fiction rather than of melodramatic opera. He had been rendered sexually incompetent by an attack of the mumps, and his Guinevere was three-quarters asleep the one time her Lancelot, the director of the opera, came to her bed wrapped in Arthur's dressing gown to demonstrate just how wrong she was when she mocked his theories about the effectiveness of disguise. All of this was too much for many reviewers who complained it was a mechanical and unrealistic forcing on life of Jungian theories of the power of myth. Davies appears certain that he is but holding a mirror up to nature. If that mirror strikes rational people as too gaudy to be true, rationalism strikes the novel's most reliable witness, Simon Darcourt, as merely "a handsomely intellectual way of sweeping a lot of significant, troublesome things under the rug."

That attitude alone is enough to render Davies suspect to people who have been influenced by—or even just intimidated by—the various clusters of theorists who have dominated American academic criticism in recent years and who are as touchily proud of their rational powers as the social scientists they are eager to emulate. Here is where Wayne Booth can be most helpful. First, he very carefully, bit by careful bit, pulls the rug out from under the arguments the theorists offer, and then, equally carefully—with an admirable willingness to appear simpleminded rather than brilliant—he sanctions a very different kind of criticism. He calls it "ethical" criticism. That's not a very satisfactory name for it, but he can't come up with a better one, nor can I. No matter, he encourages us to ignore the pretensions and jargon of semi-learned theorists and to trust the pleasure of reading fiction and of talking about it as we talk about the company we keep.

Booth's idea that any narrative, even the simplest, offers multiple roles for both the writer and the reader to play works very well with Davies's novels. Certainly Davies is well aware that behind his fictional or immediate narrator stand other narrators, each of whom is liable to be taking the others with several grains of salt; and certainly he expects his reader to be every bit as complicated and salty as he is. All three of the trilogies play complicated games between and among their various narrators and readers, and their characters, too. For a particularly glowing example I would cite *The Lyre of Orpheus*, where from the opening pages until near the end a crucial and recurring question is what to make of Simon Darcourt, the middle-aged, unmarried priest-scholar-administrator who is at the center of the novel, the pivotal figure around whom all of the plots turn. Since he is plainly a man others can and do lean on, the question is comic and unthreatening, but it remains very much alive for him, for the reader, and for the narrator (in one or two of his roles) until Darcourt comes to the realization that he is best defined by the figure of The Fool in a deck of Tarot cards. Welcoming and affirming that identity—he is a holy or blessed fool, not a damned fool—he is able to move swiftly towards resolution of the major difficulties the novel describes. That is simultaneously a nice joke and a forceful statement of central theme. That a man with a mind as large as Darcourt's should have to accept the role of The Fool is something for us to laugh about; that a man as strong as Darcourt cannot be fully effective until he recognizes that he has a well-defined, even ancient role to play is something for us to chew on. Like Arthur Cornish, and like many of the novel's reviewers, we may think that we are free to do whatever we will with our lives, but the truth is that the only freedom we have is the freedom to play the role that the myth governing the story of our lives permits us to play—or if you would prefer, as I would myself, a less Jungian, more Twainian of putting it, the freedom to play the hand we've been dealt. People who need to deny that truth can't stand to read Davies; people who can't see that as a comic truth are puzzled by him.

Davies published two more novels before he died. The second one, *The Cunning Man* (1994), strikes me as a pleasant, affable, but somewhat slack final offering. It is in the form of a memoir and like many actual memoirs it tends to ramble on, as though the writer lacked the energy to take full control of it. But *Murthers & Walking Spirits* (1991) is of a piece with his best work; it caps off many of the themes and concerns that recur through all three trilogies and, in happy addition, makes Davies himself almost explicitly the subject of fond mockery. The central business of this first-person narrative is to take the narrator, Connor Gilmartin, a man who seems to have a lot in common with Robertson Davies, down a few pegs so that he can learn to know and love his forebears, an unglamorous batch who seem to have a lot in common with Robertson Davies's forebears, so that he can finally know and love himself well enough to become a decent participant in whatever life there may be after death. The autobiographical note is struck more firmly here than in Davies's other novels; it has to be, for the game he is playing here requires that he expose himself to its risks, if only for the sake of persuading the reader to run some parallel risks of his own.

The great imperative of the comic vision of life is "Play!" Play in and with your life, in and with your work. That's hard, much harder than owlish folks can believe. Most contemporary novelists, like most of the rest of us, aren't up to anything much riskier than thumbing their noses at a few proprieties or playing a postmodernish little game of hide-and-seek. Robertson Davies started out taking more risks than that; now, near the end of his career, he has added juggling and pratfalls to his dance along the high-wire. That is to say, the narrator falls dead in the first sentence, spends most of the book watching what appear to him to be films of his forebears' lives, and finally wreaks a highly comic vengeance on his killer.

A little explanation is in order: Connor Gilmartin, Entertainment

Editor on a Toronto newspaper, finds his wife naked in bed with the paper's film critic; instead of damning her as faithless, he expresses astonishment at her poor taste in lovers. The critic, a vain, waspish man whose command of words is weak, replies with a wild swing to the temple with a cosh (in American, a blackjack) rather than with well-directed derision. Gilmartin's ghost, who can't intervene in the world of the living but can haunt, decides to follow the critic to a film festival in the hope of being able to prey on his conscience. To his astonishment, the ghostly Gilmartin sees "films" of the lives of several of the preceding generations of his forebears while the critic watches new prints of old classics. Thus, while the critic watches Eisenstein's famous propagandistic account of the Russian Revolution, *Battleship Potemkin*, he watches a totally nonideological account of his great-great-grandmother's flight in a canoe with her three children up the Hudson River valley from revolutionary New York City to Canada; and when the critic is treated to a showing of the film version of *The Master Builder* made by Ibsen's grandson Tancred in 1939, he sees his great-grandfather bankrupt himself building a massively ugly Methodist church in Salterton. In all, five private "films," each of which runs parallel to a classic film, convey wittily the stuff of an old-fashioned family-saga novel. To make matters even wittier, each of the five film chapters could be described as a novella, each of which is written in a style appropriate to novels of that time. The first one, for example, reads a lot like a good late-eighteenth-century novel of adventure, and the fourth one, which is set in the 1920s, dabbles happily in some streams of consciousness. By the end of his private viewings Gilmartin has largely rid himself of his fastidious egotism; he has not only come to accept his place in a chain of ancestors, he finds himself using more and more old-fashioned Canadian locutions. And when the time comes to take vengeance upon the critic who killed him he settles for playing a joke, singing in his ear "The bells of Hell go ting-a-ling-a-ling for you and not for me. . . ." The old-fashioned ditty does a sufficient job on the critic: the ass goes boohooing off to make a consummate ass of himself, looking for somebody who will take the load of guilt off his shoulders.

Good novelists have good minds and know it; pushed by the needs of their work they are capable of such intellectual feats as writing accurately and confidently from within the consciousness of a trooper in Cromwell's army or giving a condensed yet still accurate account of a Jungian analysis. People capable of the research, analysis, and synthesis that underlie *Prisons* and *The Manticore* do not have to shuffle modestly in the company of the most learned, most brilliant academicians. But people capable of writing such engrossing, such aesthetically compelling novels as *Prisons* and *The Manticore* do not let themselves see their intellects as anything more than useful tools, at least not while they are at work. Novelists, I think, can either tell a story or parade their fine intellectual capacities, but it seems to be not possible—to be against the laws of the form—to do both at once. Happily, what is true for good writers is true for good readers: when you submit to the discipline of reading novels like *Prisons* and *The Manticore* you submit to the highly beneficial experience of stretching your mind at the same time you are learning its comparative unimportance. Fat-headed novelists and fat-headed readers do exist, but they are a disgrace to fiction.

8

Canons, Private and Public

The nicest thing that can happen to a critic is to discover unexpectedly material that confirms the validity and usefulness of ideas he has been developing. I have had the extraordinary good fortune of having that happen more than once in the course of writing this book. I can't remember when I first began telling my students to read a poem or any other work of literature as literally as they could as long as they could; I do know that from the first moment I began thinking of the possibility of writing a book like this I had my belief in the importance of the critic of a novel being faithful to the facts of the fiction firmly connected with all that Thoreau says and shows about the importance of factual accuracy in *Walden*. I had even managed a very rough, sketchy summary of this book before I read Milan Kundera's *Testaments Betrayed* with its demonstration of the importance of reading fiction slowly and literally; I knew there was a connection between the material I planned to use in the second half of the book with the material in the first half, though I wasn't at all sure what it was or how I could explain it. Finding Kundera's reading of Hemingway's "Hills like White Elephants" while I was in the first stages of writing the fourth chapter was, as the old saying goes, like finding money from home; it showed me as clearly as anything could how to make the connection that I had been sure was there to be made. (I am, of course, referring only to Kundera's instructions on how to read; the best day I ever had I couldn't have come up with his brilliant observations about Hemingway's "melodization" of dialogue.)

Another marvelously strong confirmation of the rightness of the ideas I have been working with came a month or so ago when I got my copy of *A Book of Luminous Things*, by Czeslaw Milosz, an anthology of poems that are "loyal toward reality and attempting to describe it as concisely as possible." I had not been worrying that I was out at the end of a limb in stressing as heavily as I do the need to hold theories governing literary criticism to realistic standards and in concentrating my attention on novels in the traditions of fictional realism, but I knew—I could scarcely escape knowing—that in doing so, I was taking a distinctly unfashionable position that is frequently scorned as intellectually shabby. It came almost as a shock to find Milosz simply assuming without even arguing the matter the good sense of gathering a book full of poems that are "loyal toward reality." It should not have surprised me, for I have been savoring Milosz's work for some time, perhaps especially his poems and his lovely novel about his Lithuanian heritage, *The Issa Valley,* but also, though in a different way, his essays, his very demanding speculative work, *The Land of Ulro,* and his lucid rejection of communism, *The Captive Mind.* I even knew that in *The Witness of Poetry*—a book of lectures worth underlining if there ever was one—he defined poetry as a "passionate pursuit of the Real." Still, Milosz is such an imposing presence on the literary scene, respected by nearly all critics save the Marxists, who refuse to forgive him for having shown the rottenness of a system they have long admired from a safe distance, that I couldn't expect him to embrace as I have such a plainly "simple-minded" position. But he did, and *A Book of Luminous Things* is an extraordinary collection. With very few exceptions, all of the poems in it are clear, concise, readily accessible to an attentive reader, and a pleasure to read and to reread. I have the impression that 85 or 90 percent of them (I wasn't keeping score) were new to me, and of the ones I already knew and liked, most were poems that are not commonly anthologized and that I have liked for years. It's an anthology that meets what I think is the hardest and best test: I can open it at random and find a poem that delights me, such as "Of Rain and Air" by Wayne Dodd, a celebration of the pleasure of being out at night in a soft rain by an American poet whose work I shall have to get acquainted with.[1] I like Milosz's way of organizing the anthology in groups that cluster loosely around familiar themes but I find there's a lot to be said for working through it by nearly random selection, too. The solution is simple: read it one way once and then read it again the other way.

1. Czeslaw Milosz, *A Book of Luminous Things,* xv, 173.

When my finger landed on Dodd's poem I found on the next page another good poem on rain by another poet whose work I do not know, Sander Weores. But Weores was a Hungarian and his "Rain" comes to us in a translation by J. Kessler. That is another and even more unexpected way in which *A Book of Luminous Things* confirms the rightness of what I have been saying: half or more of the poems in the book are translations, a lot of them from Chinese, a lot more from Polish and other Slavic languages, and generous handfuls from French, Spanish, Scandinavian, and other languages. I was giving away too much when I conceded in Chapter 5 that poetry cannot be translated as successfully as novels can. Milosz has demonstrated not merely that poems of a number of different eras from a number of different languages can be translated but that our knowledge of poetry is severely diminished if we don't read those translations. I have never heard of the Japanese poet Muso Soseki (1275–1351) but thanks to W. S. Merwin, whom I have heard of, I now know that Soseki produced at least one gem of a poem, "Old Man at Leisure." "No one catches a glimpse inside his mind this old man all by himself between heaven and earth."[2] And thanks to a number of translators I have never heard of, like Reginald Gibbons, J. P. Seaton, and R. Greenwald, I now know good poems by poets who were at best faint names for me, like Jorge Guillén, Chang Chi, and Rolf Jacobsen. I am not playing at false modesty here; I really was thoroughly ignorant of most of the poets and the poetry that Milosz has introduced me to. What is more, I am certain I have a lot of company in my ignorance.

That is to say, in compiling this anthology Milosz paid no attention to the canon, to the unwritten but well-known, quasi-official list of works and writers that have such high literary quality as to be appropriate for study. He has no concern with the reputations of writers and even less concern with the classification of poetic movements; having paid his dues over the decades to the trends and fashions in the literary marketplace, he feels free to present, as an independent-minded art collector might present, a collection of works that he values, all of which center on a currently unfashionable theme. That is another way in which he gives encouraging support to what I am doing in this book. Though I mostly have not

2. Ibid., 174, 286.

been discussing the matter, I am well aware—and assume that my reader is, too—that I have been blithely ignoring both modernist and postmodernist definitions of the canon of important novels. It is time I spoke to the issue.

A great deal of silly argument that in the last five or ten years has raged over the subject of The Canon could have been avoided if the eloquent, impassioned, and (of course) highly moral partici-pants on both sides had been willing to begin with a simple dis-tinction between The Canon, a somewhat rough, tacitly accepted understanding of the works that a sound literary education should be primarily concerned with, and the uncapitalized canons of per-sonal taste and judgment that all good readers create for themselves as they go. To put it another way, The Canon is the body of litera-ture that largely defines the contents of courses of literature—the works, say, of American literature that other people will expect you to be familiar with if you claim to have some substantial knowledge of the field. Everybody who reads at all widely in the field is going to have their own personal canons, their own personal selection of the American works that they like and that others ought to know. During periods when it is thought that the content of The Canon could and should be decided solely—or apparently solely—on the basis of literary quality, general agreement on the content is easy to get, though the inclusion of this or that work may be debated. That is to say, in such periods it's fairly obvious that The Canon is simply the product of the melding of a large number of personal canons and few people are likely to be upset about their personal differ-ences with it. If the bases of personal canons undergo radical changes, as they did in the years before and after World War I, The Canon, too, will finally undergo some radical changes: the essayists, poets, and novelists highly valued by the Genteel Tradition disap-pear from popular textbooks, and Thoreau, Melville, Henry James, and T. S. Eliot become recognized as major writers. But when ide-ologies rather than aesthetic preferences tend to determine the con-tents of personal canons to the point where one can scarcely call them personal or private, as they have in the last two or three decades, then The Canon becomes the battleground for what the disputants think of as political power struggles and I think of as fantasy (because I can't believe that much real power resides in the control of the reading lists of some college courses in English). But real or fantastic, the struggles are ferocious; the proponents of this version or that of Political Correctness readily advocate depriving the Neanderthals who oppose them of tenure and the custodians of our Glorious Past would gladly run the P.C. people out of the country.

Actually, I don't think that the sense of The Canon has ever been all that strong and rigid in our universities, not in comparison with English and European universities. Americans, academic or otherwise, generally do not take to being told what is and is not worth thinking about; certainly since World War I, most of us have found some margin for experimenting in our classes and only a pitifully rigid few haven't been able to assert their own versions of the canons that make sense to them.

In concentrating as heavily as I have in this book on the novels of Josef Skvorecky, George V. Higgins, Mary Lee Settle, and Robertson Davies I am not Canoneering in the fashion of the true believers in one ideology or another—I gladly leave the composition of The Canon to the vagaries of time and fashion. I like all four of these writers very much and I'm grateful for what I have learned from them; I think anybody who likes novels would find them well worth trying. But I am not engaged in any kind of rank-ordering, to use the jargon of the opinion samplers. Of the writers I have been particularly interested in during the last ten years these are ones whose works I found I needed to write about. I have been reading other writers with care and pleasure in these years; my respect for, say, Milosz, Milan Kundera, V. S. Naipaul, Fred Chappell, George Garrett, and E. Annie Proulx is certainly high enough to encourage more reading and, with luck, some writing. Add those six to the four I have written about here and you have a list of ten names, many or most of which will raise eyebrows among critics who pride themselves on knowing who the really important writers are. Having lived long enough to have been around the block a few times, I would gently remind them that in the late 1930s practically everybody knew that John Dos Passos and John Steinbeck were major writers, at least one highly respected critic thought John P. Marquand was, too, and save for Malcolm Cowley and a few stubborn southerners nobody was saying very much at all about William Faulkner. Who knows what The Canon is or should be or will be? All that really matters is who are the writers you can enjoy not just reading but rereading. I have had a fine time rereading Skvorecky, Higgins, Settle, and Davies. (I might add, for the benefit of the curious, that though I once read them with great delight I can no longer reread either Dos Passos or Steinbeck. I don't think I could reread Marquand either, but I want to take one more look at him. I have, of course, been rereading most of Faulkner for years, and some of Malcolm Cowley, too.)

A concern for rank-ordering, either of writers or of the books of a given writer seems almost unnatural to me; certainly it's no part of the concern of children who are new to the wonders of books. They can be—usually are, I think—remarkably fussy about the books their parents read to them at bedtime; they know what they want to hear on a given night. Often it's what they have heard the last several nights in a row. They don't care what they're supposed to want and they don't care about novelty. If they like a book, they can tell right away; if they don't, you might just as well throw it away. They seem to come equipped with on-off switches. Comparative distinctions don't seem to make much sense to them. It's not that this book is better than that one, for all the books they like are books that they like. It's that this book is the one I want to hear now; tomorrow or next week can take care of themselves. As they grow older they become a little more civilized, a little less imperious in their demands; but I don't think that the ones who become habitual readers ever get over a certain childishness. How could you get totally absorbed in a book if you weren't childish or at least childlike? A responsible adult would never say, "The blazes with everything, I'm going to finish this book." Sensible children and habitual readers say it all the time, though maybe not out loud. To put it a little more politely, good readers submerge themselves in good books; insufferably brilliant readers, as I noted in the last chapter, are barred from the gates of the great novels because they cannot manage to lose themselves in mere stories. Of course, when those good readers come up for air after they have finished a book they put childishness aside and do some careful, if not brilliant, thinking.

A child's canon changes rapidly. If I remember correctly, when I was in first grade Uncle Wiggly stories were high on the list. They were soon moved aside by the Hardy Boys, sports stories by Burt L. Standish (another pen name, I have since been told, by the man responsible for the Hardy Boys), pulp fiction by Jackson V. Sholz and many others, *The Riders of the Purple Sage* and other westerns by Zane Grey, the Lawrenceville-Yale stories by a snob whose name I am glad I can't recall at the moment, Booth Tarkington's *Penrod,* and assorted barrelsful of popular fiction and nonfiction from the back shelves of libraries and from current issues of the *Saturday Evening Post.* I must have read the books librarians recommend as children's classics because I was vacuuming up everything that came my way. I do remember, though, one "good" book that for some reason I couldn't stomach, *Hans Brinker and the Silver Skates;* I don't think that I ever got past the second or third chapter of that thing. In short, no reputable educator would approve of my grade-school regimen, but it made a habitual reader out of me and gave me a chance to discover for myself, on my own terms and in my own way, the great critical truth that there is nothing quite so mysteriously satisfying as *real* writing. That is to say, when I was in fourth grade I stumbled across *Tom Sawyer* and *Huckleberry Finn.* I read all sorts of junk after that and even a few things that a sensible person might find fairly good, but having learned what twenty-four carat gold looks like I didn't get too excited about the chunks of iron pyrites that I found on the shelves of the town library.

I don't want to rehearse the whole erratic process by which my personal canon came into being; I don't think there was anything very unusual about the process or particularly eccentric about its results (perhaps because I think of myself as a perfectly normal fellow). I did learn to trust myself, especially my memory, more than any authority; that may have set me a little apart from classmates in high school and college, though not, I think, from other people who turn out to have a critical bent.

Sometime about the middle of my high school years I got hold of a collection of novels and stories by P. G. Wodehouse called *The Weekend Wodehouse.* I liked them, as I like anything that will make me laugh out loud, and over the next year or so I got from the library more Wodehouse books, especially the Jeeves stories. I read them for the pure fun of it and went off to more serious matters, World War II and college, assuming that I would grow up and forget about Wodehouse. But I never did, not even in graduate school; the memory of those stories I read when I was in high school stayed surprisingly fresh in my mind. Then I noticed that if I happened to read another one or two more, they stayed fresh as well. It wasn't until sometime in the late seventies or early eighties that it finally dawned on me that my memory was trying to tell my brain something: the Wodehouse books couldn't possibly be the trivial stuff they were commonly supposed to be; they couldn't stay so alive in my memory if they were. About the time I started to reread them critically, I got a nice supportive push from a colleague, the poet John Woods, who replied to my query if he had ever read Wodehouse by quoting with perfect accuracy the last line of *The Code of the Woosters,* "And presently the eyes closed, the muscles relaxed, the breathing became soft and regular, and sleep which does something which has slipped my mind to the something sleeve of care poured over me in a healing wave."

By the time my brain got through doing a little careful thinking about what my memory had for years been telling me, I realized that Wodehouse was a master of farce, a kind of comedy that I am positive is difficult and valuable, no matter how many owlish critics may disparage it. (If Aristophanes, Rabelais, Chaucer, Shakespeare, Molière, Fielding, Twain, Chekhov, and so forth didn't consider it beneath their dignity to exert their rare gifts to treat matters farcically, I don't know why I should pay the slightest attention to the hooting of the cultural owls.) Wodehouse's mastery is visible in a very high number of the books he published during the seventy-odd years of his productive career; for a choice sample I would cite the novel John Woods and I both fell in love with in our high-school years, *The Code of the Woosters.* It displays vividly and at moderate length his perfect tone in language and his extraordinary skill in plotting; even though it was written in 1938 it remains, I think, very funny; and it gives us what most great farce gives us, a fresh image of benign idiocy. Even readers who do not respond to its humor or dare not entertain the possibility that idiocy is a necessary restraint upon intelligence can find it instructive, for it corrects as fully as any single work can the widespread misapprehension that farce is simply a system of extravagance. *The Code of the Woosters* is as beautifully, as artfully restrained as Bach's Minuet in G; it accepts, as all of its many companions do, the constraints of the form that Wodehouse created by adapting the American musical comedy of the first quarter of the century for fiction. It must be light—"frothy," the reviewers would say—devoid of any content that anyone of a mental age beyond eight might be tempted to label *serious.* Its characters must be the simplest kind of stereotypes, and they must be various enough to supply parts for a modest-sized company of ingenues and harridans, swains and comic villains. Its young lovers must be verbally ardent and wildly jealous, without ever displaying the slightest awareness of sexuality, while its harridans and villains must be thoroughly desiccated and monomaniacal. It must be heavily plotted along recognizably conventional lines, and the plot must arrive at subclimaxes at judiciously spaced intervals. Above all it must have deft comic pace, establishing a rhythm of smiles and laughter akin to the rhythms of words and music in the great popular songs of the period. In short, it is both a demanding and a seemingly trivial form; therefore it was essential that Wodehouse never give in to the temptation to fudge on its demands or to condescend to its triviality.

Wodehousian farce, like all other kinds of farce—like most comedy, for that matter—nurses a deep suspicion that the ability to reason is an overrated gift, and what counts in farce is not originality of meaning but freshness of image. Wodehouse has given us in a beautiful amalgam of English and American language new images of idiocy so that we may realize that it is better to be sweetly stupid than aggressively brilliant. With one exception the intellectually competent people in the world he has created for us are monstrous. The women among them are relentlessly bossy, like Aunt Agatha, "who," Bertie says, "eats broken bottles and wears barbed wire next to the skin," or like Florence Craye, who plans to make a new man of Bertie and begins their engagement by making him read *Types of Ethical Theory* instead of the book he was "studying at the moment," *Blood on the Bannisters*. The competent men are even worse: they are headmasters who terrorize schoolboys, like the Reverend Aubrey Upjohn, or would-be dictators who yearn to terrorize the entire nation, like Roderick Spode. In the long run, these fiercely competent people are stupider than the nitwits they seek to crush. The exception to the Wodehousian rule that intelligence is a tool of selfishness and aggression is Jeeves. Jeeves is, in the old-fashioned phrase, "in service," and his abilities are at the command of Bertie and his friends. Jeeves is selfish only in that he will strike quickly and hard to preserve his relationship with Bertie. That relationship puzzles readers who like explanations and they suggest that Wodehouse is using it to satirize the English class system. But Wodehouse didn't have a satiric bone in his head (as Bertie might have put it), and Jeeves, who loves his little comforts, is very comfortable sitting in the kitchen reading Spinoza. I think we have to see the relationship as symbolic, as expressing Wodehouse's deepest insight—that rational intelligence becomes monstrous and ultimately self-destructive if it is not held firmly subservient to the ideals of affability and civility. Wodehouse would have us understand that Jeeves is exactly right when he tells a momentarily depressed and listless Bertie that getting the correct adjustment of his trousers always matters; for when we devote ourselves to apparently trivial things life can have gaiety, but when we take our troubles and ourselves seriously it will certainly be dreary.

Quite possibly Wodehouse saved the world from something monstrous when he devoted his own high intelligence to the making of "frothy" novels, stories, plays, and songs (he wrote the lyrics to several of Jerome Kern's best-known songs, "Leave It to Jane," "Till the Clouds Roll By," and "Bill" are among them), though he never would have entertained such a thought. Certainly he would have denied that his work embodies symbolic meanings and deep insights; he left that sort of thing to the "big shots" like Faulkner and Hemingway, and he was embarrassed by any suggestion that he might belong in their company. I wouldn't claim that he was a big shot; I wouldn't think of suggesting that he belongs in The Canon with the major writers who have shaped our literature. (Wilfred Sheed once ruefully observed that Wodehouse is the closest English and American literature have come to producing a writer of Flaubertian dedication. Sheed thinks it would be a good thing if there were more of Flaubert in our literature, as of course it would be, for Flaubert is a very big shot. But I would argue that it might be a good thing if there were more of Wodehouse in French literature, for their intellectuals do need to learn something about how to laugh at themselves.) At the same time I wouldn't think of omitting him from my personal canon of writers who have done and still are doing good things for me. How many absolutely reliable writers does one ever find, writers who never write a clumsy sentence or tell a twisted story, who manage to fuse together the best qualities of a fun-house mirror and an algebraic equation? However, as I trust I have made clear, my admiration for Wodehouse is not simply personal. Anyone who seeks to know and understand comedy in general had better read Wodehouse; if that generalized seeker becomes a specialist and wants to understand the rigorous demands and rewards of farce, a type of comedy that has remained very much alive and kicking for at least twenty-five hundred years, then some study of Wodehouse becomes a necessity.

I will cite one other happy bit of high school reading that stuck in my memory and did good things for me years later. Some time in the late winter of 1943, not long before I discovered that if I enlisted in the navy I could skip the last couple tedious months of high school and still get my diploma, I found on a shelf in the Pottstown Pennsylvania Public Library three books of autobiographical essays by somebody named H. L. Mencken called *Happy Days, Newspaper Days,* and *Heathen Days.* I grabbed all three. I didn't know Mencken from Adam, but I liked being happy, wanted to be a newspaperman, and thought of myself as a devout heathen. Furthermore, they were published by Alfred A. Knopf, and Knopf's distinctive bindings and typefaces struck me as the height of sophistication. I think I read all three of them over a single weekend, for they were not very long. I was delighted by Mencken's jaunty irreverence towards everything respectable and pious, but I drooled with envy over his prose, so clear, so direct, so marvelously assured, and so exuberant. The games he played with his huge vocabulary really fetched me. Though I was accustomed to thinking of myself as a lad with a good-sized vocabulary, he ran rings around me, frequently for the sake of a good laugh, often because it was the one right word, but never, I thought, to impress me. I had just enough sense not to try to imitate him, but I couldn't resist picking up a few of his favorite baubles for my own use, "brummagem" being the one that most annoyed my friends, and I still have a way of smacking my lips over certain preposterous words that I picked up from Mencken. I went for years hoping to have an opportunity to unload in public the phrase he used to describe an adolescent evangelist whose preachings drove him out of the local YMCA, "papuliferous exegete," but God was never that good to me.

For several years I thought that Mencken was, like Wodehouse, just a personal pleasure of mine; even in college it didn't occur to me that others might savor as much as I did those essays about growing up and getting started in a city I did not know, Baltimore, years before I was born. When I did start to hear and learn more about Mencken, it was the literary and social critic and the student of "the American language" that I heard about; the *Days* books were treated as items at the end of his bibliography, pieces of fluff that he published after the depression and Roosevelt's New Deal made his political ideas irrelevant. My memory knew better than that, but in a world in which very few people seemed to be up to thinking of Twain's "Old Times on the Mississippi" as the astonishing work of art it plainly is (or was before Twain buried it in *Life on the Mississippi*) there didn't seem to be much point in arguing that these three collections of biographical essays made Mencken an important writer in the history of American literature rather than a minor figure in American intellectual history. That memory stayed fresh through years of teaching various undergraduate writing courses and graduate as well as undergraduate courses in American literature; I would occasionally grouse because I didn't have any of the *Days* material available for class assignments, though as the years passed, recognition grew that Mencken deserved some sort of place in American literature courses. I got busy working on various projects that led to my book on the comic vision, but whenever a sales representative from Knopf would come around the department I would tell him that they ought to put out a single volume of selections from the *Days* books that I could use as a text in some courses. Nothing came of that, nor of my effort to persuade one of the younger people in the department that he could find in those books the possibility of some publications that his career badly needed. Finally, I did what I should have done years before: in the summer of 1979 I wrote to Knopf proposing that I do that one-volume selection and they accepted. It was the easiest editorial job imaginable. Once I decided to be faithful to Mencken's plan of twenty essays to a volume and to keep them in the order he followed, the essays practically selected themselves, and since he wrote with extraordinary clarity, I didn't have to fuss with explanatory notes. *A Choice of Days* was every bit as good a book as I thought it would be, almost in a class with "Old Times on the Mississippi." Mencken fully shares Twain's delight in the experience of being free and communicates it in language nearly as fresh and as humorous and yet as easy as Twain's. Unfortunately, Mencken's work is also like Twain's in not fitting into any of the categories that dominate the study of American literature; apparently the only people who can do justice to the quality of both works are people who have read a lot of Twain and a lot of Mencken. These are mostly people who read not so much to master a field as to please themselves and who therefore don't worry much about what is in or out of The Canon.

They are also people—I suppose I have to speak to this issue— who do not worry about correctness of any sort, least of all what passes for Political Correctness in our windy times. Yes, Twain did use the word *nigger* but so did everybody else in his time and place, including the people to whom the term referred. And yes, Mencken used unflattering terms to refer to Jews (especially in some journals that he thought would never be published) but so did nearly everybody else in his time and place. Yet most of the really proper people in the time and place I grew up in, the pillars of society in those prewar American towns, made it very plain to me that if I knew what I was doing I would join them in despising "those people," though speaking politely of them, of course. Neither Twain nor Mencken ever did that to me, or to anyone else; instead they persuaded me that I had the great good fortune to live in a country where everybody, myself and those near and dear to me emphatically included, gave me something to laugh at.

To go back to the much more interesting matter of the relationship between the forms (using the term loosely) of works and their selection for inclusion in The Canon of American literature, the general rule is that only works that can be fitted comfortably into one of the conventionally accepted categories of *literary* forms need apply, and it helps if they are not too long. Insofar as The Canon is a rough agreement serving the needs of teachers and departments that's understandable; shorter works in familiar forms are easiest to handle in the crowded confines of most academic courses. If you insist, as I usually did, on cramming *Moby-Dick* into a sophomore course, something else is going to have to give; Walt Whitman was such a great poet that you have to deal with him, but in an introductory course nobody can afford the time to teach more than a few selections from that single book that he thought of himself as writing. The nice thing about Emily Dickinson is that she wrote nothing but brief lyric poems, and novels as short as *The Red Badge of Courage* and *The Great Gatsby* are a comfort to one and all. Even in graduate courses long novels such as James's *The Ambassadors* and Dreiser's

An American Tragedy are troublesome, and odd works like William Carlos Williams's *Paterson* and Norman Mailer's *The Armies of the Night* are a time-consuming nuisance. Yet the truth is that we Americans are a very odd lot, much more complicated than we like to think we are—plain, simple folks, my eye—or than most European pundits are willing to admit; and it certainly would figure, then, that we would produce a literature with some very odd works in it. Our writers are like the rest of us, never quite comfortable in a category, and a remarkably large number of them produce at least one work that pushes at the boundaries separating prose and poetry or—more commonly—separating fiction from nonfiction, novels from essays and autobiographies. For openers, consider such books as *Walden* (which comes early and high on any list of our odd books), *Moby-Dick*, *The Scarlet Letter* (with its long foreword, "The Custom House"), *Leaves of Grass*, *The Education of Henry Adams*, *Life on the Mississippi*, and *Green Hills of Africa*. Or think of the writers we have had who seem to have spent most of their careers out at the edge in one way or another—Faulkner, Flannery O'Connor, Robert Penn Warren, Henry Miller (with all of what he termed his "quaint autobiographical romances"), Norman Mailer, William Carlos Williams, Cormac McCarthy, and E. Annie Proulx. I am tempted to argue, though generalizations this sweeping are rarely valid, that an American writer can't be taken as counting for very much until he or she has done a book as impractical and as hard to place as Settle's *Turkish Reflections*, Nelson Algren's *Notes of a Sea Diary: Hemingway All the Way*, George Garrett's *Poison Pen*, Ivan Doig's *Winter Brothers*, or George V. Higgins's *The Progress of the Seasons*.

Or Shelby Foote's *The Civil War: A Narrative*, a book that is precisely and exactly what its title says it is, a narrative encompassing the entire Civil War, a story—a taut, coherent story even—that happens to require three volumes of roughly a thousand pages each but that succeeds in doing for us and for that astonishingly complicated, appallingly bloody war what Homer's *Iliad* did for his Greeks and that smaller but still complicated and bloody war on the plains of Troy: it renders it *imaginable.* It can be and often is called a prose epic, for it uses most of the familiar strategies and devices of the great epics, especially in the characterizing of the major figures in the war. Lincoln and Davis, Grant and Lee, Sherman and Forrest, and many of their fellow agents in the vast struggle become vivid, larger-than-life figures that a reader can finally come to some kind of terms with, even though they are finally beyond our understanding. That is, like the major figures in all great epics, they become for us representative, almost symbolic figures, yet intensely human. Personally, however, I don't find it very helpful to put *The Civil War* in a category with the epics because for all its length and all its stress on the vastness of the conflict, it finally achieves so much of the intimacy of a novel. Foote came to this work with an established reputation as a novelist, and he exploited all of the skills he had acquired in writing *Love in a Dry Country, Shiloh, Jordan County, Follow Me Down,* and *Tournament* to make his scenes real. Yet one can scarcely categorize it as a novel either, for it is quite obviously a superbly reliable, accomplished work of history—history seen as a branch of the humanities, not of the social sciences. I would argue that *The Civil War: A Narrative* as surely belongs in The Canon as any American narrative written in the last fifty years, except that I must admit that I don't see how it could be crammed into the confines of any ordinary course in American literature, and I would quake at the thought of trying to get a classful of contemporary, history-hating students to tolerate it. At the same time, I have to insist that it makes Shelby Foote a very large figure in American literature, inescapable for any serious Americanist. *Shiloh* and *September, September* are fine novels well worth rereading, but *The Civil War* is that marvelous something else again that helps us understand who and what we are.

If I can't claim that all significant American writers sooner or later produce formally odd books that defy categorization because that "all" is too sweeping, I am certainly justified in arguing that anybody who wants to know our literature had better get used to finding it in unexpected forms and places; that's what makes canon-making here so difficult. My own prize illustration of this truth is a book called *The Glory of Their Times* by Lawrence Ritter. The book is, of all things, a gathering of interviews with old-time baseball players, and the writer is, of all things, an economist of very substantial reputation. More exactly, the book is a compilation of skillfully edited transcripts of interviews with surviving representatives of the generation of players who flourished in the big leagues before and after World War I that were conducted between

1962 and 1966 by a man who was both baseball fan and scholar enough to realize the value, and urgency, of getting their stories on tape. The results are extraordinary. Ritter gives the credit to the players, "a group of friendly and intelligent men who were not only delighted to talk about their experiences, but who were also able to articulate them in such a way as to bring them vividly alive today, often a half century or more after the fact. They re-created their lives and those of their contemporaries with warmth, insight and compassion. They told their stories with pride and with dignity, and also with joy."[3] But Ritter deserves a generous share of the credit, too. He has a gift for interviewing that would put nearly all contemporary sports journalists to shame: he didn't so much ask questions as prompt the men to keep on talking, and he had both the ear and the intelligence to relish their way of talking. "Listen," he tells you at the end of his preface, and you can *hear* every word they say. You hear nothing of Ritter, for he had the great good sense to do what no journalist could afford to do, he edited himself clean out of the book. Colleagues who are not themselves baseball fans are prone to deny my claim that *The Glory of Their Times* is a work of literature—journalism, yes; maybe even social history, but not literature. Yet what else can I call a book that gives me twenty-two distinctly different characters who have a gift for telling not only stories about their own lives but the story of their times as well? Baseball is a distinctly American enterprise and the dream of playing in the big leagues is a distinctively American dream; in talking about their careers Rube Marquard, Tommy Leach, Davy Jones, Wahoo Sam Crawford, and the other eighteen tell a very great deal about the America of their times. I know of a lot of frequently admired novels, poems, and plays, all classed as literature, that fall well short of *The Glory of Their Times* in the force of their language and the quality of their stories. I value it accordingly.

I could go on for some time discussing candidates for my private little Hall of Distinguished American Oddities, for I have had the good luck that comes from trusting hunches enough to read a few unlikely looking books now and again. But I want to return to the note on which this chapter began, the unexpected discovery of material confirming the soundness of ideas that I have been working

3. Lawrence Ritter, *The Glory of Their Times*, xvii.

with in writing this book, specifically comments by some people who meet the Twainian test of knowing what they are talking about supporting or even amplifying what I have been saying about the nature and importance of stories.

Edward Chalfant first. I have greatly admired the two books that he has published about Henry Adams, *Both Sides of the Ocean,* which covers the years 1838–1862, and *Better in Darkness, 1862–1891;* each is labeled "A Biography of Henry Adams," and a third volume covering the remaining years until his death in 1918 is in the offing. I find that label on the dust jacket and title pages misleading, for what I have been reading seems nothing like installments in a multivolume biography. The term used in the preface, "a trilogy," makes better sense to me, but how should I refer to these very interesting books when I am telling others about them? If it's a trilogy, what kind of trilogy is it? When I wrote to Chalfant asking how he referred to them, the answer was energetic, as though no one had ever asked him that question before, and surprising. "If asked what I am, I'm likely to say 'a biographer' or 'a research biographer.' But you are right. The books are not biographies, and I am not a member of the biographer tribe. Not that I have anything against biographies or biographers. I don't. Yet the truth about the books and about me has to lie in some other area." Then he proceeds to tell a story about a snowy night in the mid-1970s when he was living on the corner of Eighty-fourth Street and Madison Avenue and went out for a little exercise. He found himself by the little pond in Central Park opposite East Seventy-fifth Street looking at the bronze statue of Hans Christian Andersen sitting with a book on his knee opened to the beginning of "The Ugly Duckling" (in English). "Wanting to give him something, I made a well-packed, well-rounded snowball and perched it on his book, in case he had use for it, maybe for tossing good-naturedly at the next person who came along. There," he says, "you have the essence of the whole matter."

There, I would say, you have a fine scholar, who has devoted his career first to researching every nook and cranny of the life of Henry Adams and then to writing an astonishing trilogy of books that "are not biographies" about the life of that man who is often (albeit foolishly) thought of as the frostiest man of letters in America in the eighty years between 1838 and 1918, explaining the essence of his life's work by telling how he once made a snowball in tribute to world's greatest teller of stories for children. That takes some explaining. "I have no loyalties to biography, or the novel, the short story, drama, history, the essay—none even to poetry, or ballet—as forms. Perhaps I am primitive. What matters to me is the best-ever stories. I mean ones like *The Scarlet Letter* whose reality is real throughout and cannot be doubted." He says that when he first started work on Adams in 1941 he sensed a best-ever story was implicit in the material. In the summer of 1955, a year after he was awarded the Ph.D., he realized that the story could be told only if it were presented in short episodes. In 1962 he learned to his satisfaction "that the story would fall out in three books, each in three parts made up of nine chapters, making eighty-one chapters in all. That's exactly the way it is coming out." At the time of writing the letter he was in part 3 of the last book, "finishing Chapter 19, with eight chapters still to go." Dr. Edward Chalfant may be a Professor Emeritus with numerous publications and honors, but Ed Chalfant sees himself simply as a storyteller, trying as a good storyteller should to "complete the story in plain language with all possible concision, excluding nothing essential." He doesn't even think of it as being written: "My tendency instead is to get it told. All its rhythms are rhythms of speech."[4]

Chalfant's account of himself and his work suggests that when I was arguing from the example of novelists in my fourth chapter that storytelling is a powerful way *of thinking* I was in effect understating the case; scholarship as well as fiction, drama, and poetry can be grounded in a strong sense of the story. That is not the sort of point that can be proven, but another distinguished Professor Emeritus, Louis D. Rubin Jr., gives at least indirect support to it in an account of himself that he published under the title "Criticism and Fiction: Observations by a Jackleg Practitioner." His essay is primarily concerned with the fact that in the forty-five years he has been writing professionally he has been a novelist as well as a critic. He doesn't really see the writing of fiction and of criticism as two independent enterprises; for him they are linked, if not fused, actions. "I have written the kind of fiction that I do for the same underlying impulses that have been responsible for my having

4. Edward Chalfant, letter to the author, March 2, 1997.

written my particular kind of criticism." For him, either kind of writing is a way of thinking. "We don't write merely in order to communicate; we also do it in order to find out what we know." Much later in the essay—after some interesting discussion of ways in which criticism can misunderstand how ideas and purposes the novelist isn't aware of having can shape fiction, and of ways in which the novelist's work can be damaged by an excess of the kind of conscious, rational purposes critics are comfortable with—he concludes that "whether as critics or as novelists, we write about what we care about."[5] Good scientists have taken to correcting the high-schoolish account of science as a steadily rational, logical, inductive enterprise by explaining that first they get their hunches (or insights or ideas, if you want a dressier term for it) and then they go to work testing them in numerous experiments. It's too bad that more scholars in the humanities don't feel free to admit how dreamy the origins of their scholarship are. First come their hunches, their ideas of the stories that need to be told, and then comes the careful, rational work of amassing the evidence that supports them.

Nobody, as I have insisted before, knows where those hunches or ideas or stories come from any more than original humorists know where their jokes come from. The universal testimony of those who are willing to talk about such a risky matter—theorizing about what makes your work tick might well stop it from ticking—is that the hunches come unbidden, that they themselves have practically nothing to do with it. One minute they don't have the idea; the next minute they do. Jokers often feel like innocent bystanders; they don't know they are in possession of a joke until they hear themselves saying it. They are surprised in the same way that poets are surprised by the metaphors that suddenly come into their heads or onto their pages. The stories that good writers write, in whatever form they happen to be writing, are given to them; hack writers, like mediocre comedians, plodding scientists, and dull scholars, tell the stories they figure they are supposed to tell. I should add, of course, that the best hunches, ideas, stories, and jokes are given only to people who have done a great deal of work to prepare for them and who stand ready to do a massive amount of work to

5. Rubin, "Criticism and Fiction," 205, 206, 223.

develop them. The mad scientist/artist/scholar of popular myth does not exist; but all of the good ones do what strikes ordinary folks as an insane amount of work in exploiting the implications inherent in what the fates have given them.

When I sent George Higgins a copy of my sixth chapter (because I had to get his approval of the use I was making of his letters to me) I was a trifle apprehensive about how he might respond to my repeated insistence that the story comes to the novelist as a given, as something he is more responsible to than responsible for. I hoped it didn't look like I was suggesting that he didn't really know what he was doing in writing those twenty-some novels of his. I shouldn't have worried. It turns out that once again I had been understating the case. That is to say, he replied by sending me a copy of a rough draft of an essay he is working on intermittently (in the periods when he is not actively at work on a novel) under the title "Real Time and Writing Time."[6] In it he explains that his stories come to him at odd and unexpected times, never when he's at the keyboard, always when he's away from his desk doing the odd jobs of daily life or enjoying the small pleasures, eating, driving, sailing, and so forth. It always begins with one of what turns out to be a cast of characters, not necessarily the protagonist, arriving within earshot and talking. Higgins says that he must immediately begin taking careful note of what is said on one of the several pieces of notepaper he always carries with him; if he doesn't get it now he'll never have another chance. For some considerable while his job is to listen to what his characters are saying not so much to him as to each other; if they tend to do a lot of their talking around four o'clock in the morning when he gets up to go to the bathroom, as aging males must, and keep him awake until six, that's his problem. This means that he does not plan a novel; he listens to what his characters say, watches what they do, and records it all as best he can.

"The *happening* of stories is never logically evident in the course of their first development." He says that he was approaching the end of the final draft of *Defending Billy Ryan* before he learned that Jerry Kennedy's great victory in that case may have been rigged by his unscrupulous friend and sometime client, Teddy Franklin, be-

6. George V. Higgins, letter to the author, March 28, 1997.

cause Teddy hadn't said so until then. Or again, he says it was late in the writing of *Victories* that he discovered the crucial development that much of the story hinges on, the death of Henry Briggs's unbeatable opponent, the longtime incumbent congressman from his district, just before the election. *Bomber's Law* looks like, and is, a beautifully tight account of how its hero, Detective Sergeant Harry Dell'Appa, gradually built a case against the novel's crooked cop, but Higgins says that none of the building blocks of the case was evident to him until he found out about it and promptly wrote it down. The example that most astonishes me comes from *Sandra Nichols Found Dead*. I normally would take the last chapter, in which Jerry Kennedy finally figures out how he can win the children's suit for damages for the wrongful death of their mother, as a particularly nice illustration of how a good novelist can manage his material so as to swiftly and credibly bring a complicated story to resolution, but Higgins testifies that he never was certain of how that case could end satisfactorily—it was Jerry Kennedy who found the way to do it, not him.

I hope no one will take Higgins too literally here. Starvation awaits any poor fool of a would-be writer who thinks he can hang around twiddling his thumbs until he hears voices telling him what to write—or worse, sets his alarm clock to wake him up in the middle of the night so he doesn't miss any inspiration. Neither Higgins nor any other sensible writer trusts to inspiration. Higgins, who was a successful newspaperman and lawyer before he became a novelist, has all the intellectual capacities that he would need to concoct plausible books, but in those earlier incarnations he learned to listen, really listen, to what people said and to respond to the covert as well as the overt significance of what they were saying. Thus he doesn't need to stoop to concoction; he can trust his imagination to tell him—quite literally tell him—what he needs to comprehend. It's not so very different from what Henry James did, listening to the conversations at all those dinner parties in London for the "germs" of his stories; it's just that Higgins is not nearly so sociable as James was and has to hallucinate the talk he overhears. Of the many ways of fulfilling the obligation to listen to "the wisdom of the novel," as Kundera calls it, Higgins's is just one of the more spectacular.

Then there is Edward O. Wilson on the paramount importance of storytelling in his autobiography, *Naturalist*. "Unlike experimental biologists, evolutionary biologists well versed in natural history already have an abundance of answers from which to pick and choose. What they most need are the right questions. The most important evolutionary biologists are those who invent the most important questions. They look for the best stories Nature has to tell us, because they are above all storytellers. If they are also naturalists—and a great majority of the best evolutionary biologists are naturalists—they go into the field with open eyes and minds, complete opportunists looking in all directions for the big questions, the main chance."[7]

Finally, Lewis Thomas. In one of the essays gathered in his last collection, *The Fragile Species*, he discusses the implications of an important series of experiments conducted in the early 1950s under the direction of James Olds that demonstrated the existence near the medial forebrain of rats a narrow bundle of fibers that when stimulated would produce pure pleasure that seemed wholly unrelated to any of their needs. The rats would stand for hours happily pushing the treadle that delivered the stimulation and ignoring such minor matters as food, sleep, and sex. This was the heyday of behavioral psychology when "drives" were everything, and pleasure, like consciousness, simply wasn't supposed to exist. But Olds and his colleagues kept investigating this "pleasure center" and soon other neurobiologists around the world were looking for and finding pleasure centers in other animals up to and including human beings. It was a hot topic for quite a few years, Thomas says, though no one knew quite what to do with what they were finding. In the late 1970s they stopped talking about pleasure or pleasure centers or pleasure stimulation, which are all value-laden conceptual terms, and referred to the simply technical matter of Intracranial Self-Stimulation (ICSS, naturally); by the mid-1980s they weren't talking about the phenomenon at all. Apparently, skilled research of the conventional reductionist kind had gone about as far as it could with it. Thomas, who dearly loves speculation of this sort, takes it to mean that "there is such a thing as pure pleasure, and there is a mechanism for mediating it alive in our brains." He

7. Edward O. Wilson, *Naturalist*, 167.

goes further and argues that the pleasure is the sense of being alive. "Pleasure in being alive *ought* to exist as a special, independent, autonomous sense."[8] That's the meaning he derives from the biological sciences from Darwin on down and—equally—from the music of Beethoven and Bach.

I would simply add that I derive that same meaning from *Walden* and observe that the arts in general and literature in particular, alone among human endeavors, have the function of giving pleasure while at the same time expressing a vision. That's why we tell stories—to make sense and to stay alive.

8. Lewis Thomas, *The Fragile Species*, 34–35.

Bibliography

Berman, Paul. "Paris Follies." *New Yorker*, February 1, 1993, 103–6.

Booth, Wayne C. *The Company We Keep: An Ethics of Fiction.* Berkeley and Los Angeles: University of California Press, 1988.

Cameron, Donald. *Conversations with Canadian Novelists, Part 1.* Toronto: Macmillan, 1973.

Carroll, Joseph. *Evolution and Literary Theory.* Columbia: University of Missouri Press, 1995.

Carter, Angela. "A Magical Moment in Prague." *New York Times Book Review*, February 10, 1991, 1, 36.

Cervantes, Miguel de. *The Ingenious Gentleman Don Quixote de La Mancha.* Trans. Samuel Putnam. New York: Viking, 1954.

Coetzee, J. M. "Only in Amerika." *New York Review of Books*, October 3, 1996, 12–15.

Coles, Robert. *The Call of Stories: Teaching and the Moral Imagination.* Boston: Houghton, Mifflin, 1989.

Cozzens, James Gould. *Guard of Honor.* New York: Harcourt, Brace, 1948.

Davies, Robertson. *The Cunning Man.* Toronto: McClelland and Stewart, 1994.

———. *Fifth Business.* New York: Viking, 1970.

———. *High Spirits.* New York: Viking, 1983.

———. *Hunting Stuart and Other Plays.* Toronto: New Press, 1972.

———. *Leaven of Malice.* New York: Charles Scribner's Sons, 1955.

———. *The Lyre of Orpheus.* New York: Viking, 1989.

———. *The Manticore.* New York: Viking, 1972.

———. *The Mirror of Nature.* Toronto: University of Toronto Press, 1983.

———. *A Mixture of Frailties.* New York: Scribner's, 1958.

———. *Murther and Walking Spirits.* Toronto: McClelland and Stewart, 1991.

———. *The Papers of Samuel Marchbanks*. New York: Viking, 1986.

———. *Reading and Writing*. Salt Lake City: University of Utah Press, 1992.

———. *The Rebel Angels*. New York: Viking, 1982.

———. *Tempest-Tost*. Toronto: Clarke, Irwin, 1951.

———. *World of Wonders*. New York: Viking, 1976.

De Man, Paul. *Wartime Journalism: 1940–1942*. Ed. Werner Hamacher, Neil Hertz, and Tom Keenan. Lincoln: University of Nebraska Press, 1989.

Donoghue, Denis. *Ferocious Alphabets*. Boston: Little, Brown, 1981.

Edelman, Gerald M. *Bright Air, Brilliant Fire: On the Matter of the Mind*. New York: Basic Books, 1992.

Falck, Colin. *Myth, Truth, and Literature*. 2d ed. Cambridge: Cambridge University Press, 1994.

Fischbach, Gerald D. *Mind and Brain: A Scientific American Special Report*. New York: Scientific American, 1994.

Fish, Stanley. "Professor Sokal's Bad Joke." *New York Times*, May 21, 1996.

Foote, Shelby. *The Civil War: A Narrative*. 3 vols. New York: Vintage Books, 1986.

Garrett, George. *Understanding Mary Lee Settle*. Columbia: University of South Carolina Press, 1988.

Gross, Paul R., and Norman Levitt. *Higher Superstition: The Academic Left and Its Quarrels with Science*. Baltimore: Johns Hopkins University Press, 1994.

Hamacher, Werner, Neil Hertz, and Tom Keenan, eds. *Responses: On Paul de Man's Wartime Journalism*. Lincoln: University of Nebraska Press, 1989.

Hawking, Stephen. *A Brief History of Time*. New York: Bantam Books, 1988.

Higgins, George V. *Bomber's Law*. New York: Henry Holt, 1993.

———. *A Change of Gravity*. New York: Henry Holt, 1997.

———. *A Choice of Enemies*. New York: Alfred A. Knopf, 1984.

———. *A City on a Hill*. New York: Alfred A. Knopf, 1975.

———. *Cogan's Trade*. New York: Alfred A. Knopf, 1974.

———. *Defending Billy Ryan*. New York: Henry Holt, 1992.

———. *The Digger's Game*. New York: Alfred A. Knopf, 1973

———. *Dreamland*. Boston: Little, Brown, 1977.

———. *The Friends of Eddie Coyle*. New York: Alfred A. Knopf, 1972.

————. *The Friends of Richard Nixon.* Boston: Little, Brown, 1975.

————. *Impostors.* New York: Henry Holt, 1986.

————. *The Judgment of Deke Hunter.* Boston: Little, Brown, 1976.

————. *Kennedy for the Defense.* New York: Alfred A. Knopf, 1980.

————. *The Mandeville Talent.* New York: Henry Holt, 1991.

————. *On Writing: Advice for Those Who Write to Publish (or Would Like To).* New York: Henry Holt, 1990.

————. *Outlaws.* New York: Henry Holt, 1987.

————. *The Patriot Game.* New York: Alfred A. Knopf, 1982.

————. *Penance for Jerry Kennedy.* New York: Alfred A. Knopf, 1985.

————. *The Progress of the Seasons: Forty Years of Baseball in Our Town.* New York: Henry Holt, 1989.

————. *The Rat on Fire.* New York: Alfred A. Knopf, 1981.

————. *Sandra Nichols Found Dead.* New York: Henry Holt, 1996.

————. *The Sins of the Fathers.* London: André Deutsch, 1988.

————. *Style vs. Substance: Boston, Kevin White, and the Politics of Illusion.* New York: Macmillan, 1984.

————. *Swan Boats at Four.* New York: Henry Holt, 1995.

————. *Trust.* New York: Henry Holt, 1989.

————. *Victories.* New York: Henry Holt, 1990.

————. *Wonderful Years, Wonderful Years.* New York: Henry Holt, 1988.

————. *A Year or So with Edgar.* New York: Harper and Row, 1979.

Hobson, J. Allan. *The Chemistry of Conscious States: How the Brain Changes Its Mind.* Boston: Little, Brown, 1994.

Howe, Irving. Introduction to *The Castle,* by Franz Kafka, trans. Willa Muir and Edwin Muir. New York: Schocken Books, 1992.

Judt, Tony. *Past Imperfect: French Intellectuals, 1944–1956.* Berkeley and Los Angeles: University of California Press, 1992.

Koestler, Arthur. *The Act of Creation.* New York: Dell, 1967.

Kundera, Milan. *The Art of the Novel.* Trans. Linda Asher. New York: HarperCollins, 1986.

————. "Preface to the French Edition of *Mirakl (The Miracle Game).*" In *The Achievement of Josef Skvorecky,* ed. Sam Solecki. Toronto: University of Toronto Press, 1994.

————. *Testaments Betrayed: An Essay in Nine Parts.* Trans. Linda Asher. New York: HarperCollins, 1995.

Lederman, Leon (with Dick Teresi). *The God Particle: If the Universe Is the Answer, What Is the Question?* Boston: Houghton Mifflin, 1993.

Lehman, David. *Signs of the Times: Deconstruction and the Fall of Paul de Man.* New York: Poseidon Press, 1992.

Mayr, Ernst. *This Is Biology: The Science of the Living World.* Cambridge: Harvard University Press, Belknap Press, 1997.

McCormick, John. "Down with Translation." *Sewanee Review* 104 (1996): lxviii–lxx.

Meyers, Jeffrey. *Hemingway, a Biography.* New York: Harper and Row, 1985.

Milosz, Czeslaw, ed. *A Book of Luminous Things: An International Anthology of Poetry.* New York: Harcourt, Brace, 1996.

Penrose, Roger. *The Emperor's New Mind: Concerning Computers, Minds, and the Laws of Physics.* New York: Oxford University Press, 1989.

———. *Shadows of the Mind: A Search for the Missing Science of Consciousness.* New York: Oxford University Press, 1994.

Penrose, Roger, with Abner Shimony, Nancy Cartwright, and Stephen Hawking. *The Large, the Small, and the Human Mind.* Cambridge: Cambridge University Press, 1997.

Percy, Walker. *The Message in the Bottle: How Queer Man Is, How Queer Language Is, and What One Has to Do with the Other.* New York: Farrar, Straus, Giroux, 1975.

Pinker, Steven. *The Language Instinct: How the Mind Creates Language.* New York: Harper, 1995.

Ritter, Lawrence. *The Glory of Their Times.* New York: Macmillan, 1966.

Rubin, Louis D., Jr. "Criticism and Fiction: Observations by a Jackleg Practitioner." *Virginia Quarterly Review* 73 (1997): 204–24.

Saussure, Ferdinand de. *Course in General Linguistics.* Trans. Wade Baskin; ed. Charles Bally and Albert Sechehaye. New York: Philosophical Library, 1959.

Searle, John R. "The Mystery of Consciousness, Part 1." *New York Review of Books,* November 2, 1995, 60–66.

———. "The Mystery of Consciousness, Part 2." *New York Review of Books,* November 16, 1995, 54–61.

———. *The Rediscovery of the Mind.* Cambridge: MIT Press, 1992.

Settle, Mary Lee. *All the Brave Promises: Memories of Aircraft Woman 2nd Class 2146391.* New York: Scribner's, 1988.

———. *Blood Tie.* New York: Scribner's, 1986.

———. *Celebration.* New York: Farrar, Straus, Giroux, 1986.

———. *Charley Bland*. New York: Farrar, Straus, Giroux, 1989.

———. *Choices*. New York: Doubleday, 1995.

———. *The Clam Shell*. New York: Scribner's, 1987.

———. *The Killing Ground*. New York: Scribner's, 1988.

———. *The Kiss of Kin*. New York: Scribner's, 1986.

———. *Know Nothing*. New York: Scribner's, 1988.

———. *The Love Eaters*. New York: Scribner's, 1986.

———. *O Beulah Land*. New York: Scribner's, 1987.

———. *Prisons*. New York: Scribner's, 1987.

———. *The Scapegoat*. New York: Scribner's, 1988.

———. "The Search for Beulah Land: The Story behind *The Beulah Quintet*." New York: Scribner's, 1988.

———. *Turkish Reflections: A Biography of a Place*. New York: Prentice Hall, 1991.

Skvorecky, Josef. *The Bass Saxophone*. Trans. Kaca Polackova Henley. New York: Washington Square Press, 1985.

———. *The Bride of Texas: A Romantic Tale from the Real World*. Trans. Kaca Polackova Henley. Toronto: Alfred A. Knopf, 1995.

———. *The Cowards*. Trans. Jeanne Němcová. New York: Ecco Press, 1980.

———. *Dvorak in Love*. Trans. Paul Wilson. Toronto: Lester and Orpen Dennys, 1986.

———. *The End of Lieutenant Boruvka*. Trans. Paul Wilson. New York: W. W. Norton, 1990.

———. *The Engineer of Human Souls*. Trans. Paul Wilson. New York: Alfred A. Knopf, 1984.

———. *Headed for the Blues: A Memoir*. Trans. Kaca Polackova Henley. New York: Ecco Press, 1996.

———. *The Miracle Game*. Trans. Paul Wilson. Toronto: Lester and Orpen Dennys, 1990.

———. *Miss Silver's Past*. Trans. Peter Kussi. New York: Ecco Press, 1985.

———. *The Mournful Demeanour of Lieutenant Boruvka*. Trans. Rosemary Kavan, Kaca Polackova, and George Theiner. New York: W. W. Norton, 1987.

———. *The Republic of Whores*. Trans. Paul Wilson. Toronto: Alfred A. Knopf, 1993.

———. *The Return of Lieutenant Boruvka*. Trans. Paul Wilson. Toronto: Lester and Orpen Dennys, 1990.

———. *Sins for Father Knox*. Trans. Kaca Polackova Henley. Toronto: Lester and Orpen Dennys, 1988.

———. *The Swell Season: A Text on the Most Important Things in Life*. Trans. Paul Wilson. Don Mills: Totem Press, 1985.

———. *Talkin' Moscow Blues*. Ed. Sam Solecki. New York: Ecco Press, 1990.

———. *The Tenor Saxophonist's Story*. Trans. Caleb Crain, Kaca Polackva, and Peter Kussi. New York: Ecco Press, 1996.

Sokal, Alan. "A Physicist Experiments with Cultural Studies." *Lingua Franca*, May/June 1996, 62–64.

———. "Transgressing the Boundaries: Toward a Transformative Hermeneutics of Quantum Gravity." *Social Text* 46/47 (Spring/Summer 1996): 217–52.

Sturrock, John. "The Last Days of the Intellocrats." *New York Times Book Review*, January 10, 1993, 1, 25.

Thomas, Lewis. *The Fragile Species*. New York: Macmillan, 1992.

Thoreau, Henry David. *Walden and Civil Disobedience*. Ed. Owen Thomas. New York: Norton, 1966.

Vickers, Brian. *Appropriating Shakespeare: Contemporary Critical Quarrels*. New Haven: Yale University Press, 1993.

Weightman, John. "Fatal Attraction." *New York Review of Books*, February 11, 1993, 9–12.

Wills, Garry. *Lincoln at Gettysburg: The Words That Remade America*. New York: Simon and Schuster, 1992.

Wilson, Edward O. *Naturalist*. New York: Warner Books, 1995.

Wister, Owen. *The Virginian*. New York: Grosset and Dunlap, 1911.

Wodehouse, P. G. *The Code of the Woosters*. New York: Random House, 1975.

———. *The World of Jeeves*. New York: Harper and Row, 1968.

Woodcock, George. "The Unforgivable Sin of Ignorance: Notes on *The Engineer of Human Souls*." In *The Achievement of Josef Skvorecky*, ed. Sam Solecki. Toronto: University of Toronto Press, 1994.

Index